CBSE Term II
2022

Sociology

Class XI

CBSE Term II 2022

Sociology

Class XI

- Complete Theory Covering NCERT
- Case Based Questions
- Short/Long Answer Type Questions
- 3 Practice Papers with Explanations

Authors
Dinu Mol Varkey
Raj Priya Verma

ARIHANT PRAKASHAN (School Division Series)

CBSE Term II
2022

ARIHANT PRAKASHAN (School Division Series)

 **Administrative & Production Offices**

Regd. Office
'Ramchhaya' 4577/15, Agarwal Road, Darya Ganj, New Delhi -110002
Tele: 011- 47630600, 43518550

Head Office
Kalindi, TP Nagar, Meerut (UP) - 250002, Tel: 0121-7156203, 7156204

Sales & Support Offices
Agra, Ahmedabad, Bengaluru, Bareilly, Chennai, Delhi, Guwahati, Hyderabad, Jaipur, Jhansi, Kolkata, Lucknow, Nagpur & Pune.

ISBN : 978-93-25796-85-0

PRICE : ₹125.00

PO No : TXT-XX-XXXXXXX-X-XX

Published by Arihant Publications (India) Ltd.

For further information about the books published by Arihant, log on to www.arihantbooks.com or e-mail at info@arihantbooks.com

Follow us on   

Contents

Watch Free Learning Videos

Subscribe **arihant** You**Tube** Channel

☑ Video Solutions of CBSE Sample Papers
☑ Chapterwise Important MCQs
☑ CBSE Updates

Syllabus

CBSE Term II Class XI

No.	Units	Marks
1.	Social Change and Social Order in Rural and Urban Society	14
2.	Introducing Western Sociologists	14
3.	Indian Sociologists	12
	Total	**40**

CBSE Circular

Acad – 51/2021, 05 July 2021

Exam Scheme Term I & II

केन्द्रीय माध्यमिक शिक्षा बोर्ड

(शिक्षा मंत्रालय, भारत सरकार के अधीन एक स्वायत संगठन)

CENTRAL BOARD OF SECONDARY EDUCATION

(An Autonomous Organisation under the Ministryof Education, Govt. of India)

CBSE/DIR (ACAD)/2021

Date: July 05, 2021
Circular No: Acad-51/2021

All the Heads of Schools affiliated to CBSE

Subject: Special Scheme of Assessment for Board Examination Classes X and XII for the Session 2021-22

COVID 19 pandemic caused almost all CBSE schools to function in a virtual mode for most part of the academic session of 2020-21. Due to the extreme risk associated with the conduct of Board examinations during the second wave in April 2021, CBSE had to cancel both its class X and XII Board examinations of the year 2021 and results are to be declared on the basis of a credible, reliable, flexible and valid alternative assessment policy. This, in turn, also necessitated deliberations over alternative ways to look at the learning objectives as well as the conduct of the Board Examinations for the academic session 2021-22 in case the situation remains unfeasible.

CBSE has also held stake holder consultations with Government schools as well as private independent schools from across the country especially schools from the remote rural areas and a majority of them have requested for the rationalization of the syllabus, similar to last year in view of reduced time permitted for organizing online classes. The Board has also considered the concerns regarding differential availability of electronic gadgets, connectivity and effectiveness of online teaching and other socio-economic issues specially with respect to students from economically weaker section and those residing in far flung areas of the country. In a survey conducted by CBSE, it was revealed that the rationalized syllabus notified for the session 2020-21 was effective for schools in covering the syllabus and helped learners in achieving learning objectives in a less stressful manner.

In the above backdrop and in line with the Board's continued focus on assessing stipulated learning outcomes by making the examinations competencies and core concepts based, student-centric, transparent, technology-driven, and having advance provision of alternatives for different future scenarios, the following schemes are introduced for the Academic Session for Class X and Class XII 2021-22.

केन्द्रीय माध्यमिक शिक्षा बोर्ड

(शिक्षा मंत्रालय, भारत सरकार के अधीन एक स्वायत संगठन)

CENTRAL BOARD OF SECONDARY EDUCATION

(An Autonomous Organisation under the Ministryof Education, Govt. of India)

Special Scheme for 2021-22

A. Academic session to be divided into 2 Terms with approximately 50% syllabus in each term:

The syllabus for the Academic session 2021-22 will be divided into 2 terms by following a systematic approach by looking into the interconnectivity of concepts and topics by the Subject Experts and the Board will conduct examinations at the end of each term on the basis of the bifurcated syllabus. This is done to increase the probability of having a Board conducted classes X and XII examinations at the end of the academic session.

B. The syllabus for the Board examination 2021-22 will be rationalized similar to that of the last academic session to be notified in July 2021. For academic transactions, however, schools will follow the curriculum and syllabus released by the Board vide Circular no. F.1001/CBSE-Acad/Curriculum/2021 dated 31 March 2021. Schools will also use alternative academic calendar and inputs from the NCERT on transacting the curriculum.

C. Efforts will be made to make Internal Assessment/ Practical/ Project work more credible and valid as per the guidelines and Moderation Policy to be announced by the Board to ensure fair distribution of marks.

Details of Curriculum Transaction

- Schools will continue teaching in distance mode till the authorities permit in-person mode of teaching in schools.

- **Classes IX-X: Internal Assessment** (throughout the year-irrespective of Term I and II) would include the *3 periodic tests, student enrichment, portfolio and practical work/ speaking listening activities/ project.*

- **Classes XI-XII: Internal Assessment** (throughout the year-irrespective of Term I and II) would include end of topic or unit tests/ exploratory activities/ practicals/ projects.

- Schools would create a student profile for all assessment undertaken over the year and retain the evidences in digital format.

- CBSE will facilitate schools to upload marks of Internal Assessment on the CBSE IT platform.

- Guidelines for Internal Assessment for all subjects will also be released along with the rationalized term wise divided syllabus for the session 2021-22.The Board would also provide additional resources like sample assessments, question banks, teacher training etc. for more reliable and valid internal assessments.

केन्द्रीय माध्यमिक शिक्षा बोर्ड

(शिक्षा मंत्रालय, भारत सरकार के अधीन एक स्वायत संगठन)

CENTRAL BOARD OF SECONDARY EDUCATION

(An Autonomous Organisation under the Ministryof Education, Govt. of India)

Term I Examinations:

- At the end of the first term, the Board will organize **Term I Examination** in a flexible schedule to be conducted between November-December 2021 with a window period of 4-8 weeks for schools situated in different parts of country and abroad. Dates for conduct of examinations will be notified subsequently.

- The Question Paper will have Multiple Choice Questions (MCQ) including case-based MCQs and MCQs on assertion-reasoning type. Duration of test will be **90 minutes** and it will cover only the rationalized syllabus of **Term I only** (i.e. approx. 50% of the entire syllabus).

- Question Papers will be sent by the CBSE to schools along with marking scheme.

- The exams will be conducted under the supervision of the External Center Superintendents and Observers appointed by CBSE.

- The responses of students will be captured on OMR sheets which, after scanning may be directly uploaded at CBSE portal or alternatively may be evaluated and marks obtained will be uploaded by the school on the very same day. The final direction in this regard will be conveyed to schools by the Examination Unit of the Board.

- Marks of the **Term I** Examination will contribute to the final overall score of students.

Term II Examination/ Year-end Examination:

- At the end of the second term, the Board would organize **Term II or Year-end Examination** based on the rationalized syllabus of Term II only (i.e. approximately 50% of the entire syllabus).

- This examination would be held around **March-April 2022** at the examination centres fixed by the Board.

- The paper will be of **2 hours duration** and have questions of different formats (case-based/ situation based, open ended- short answer/ long answer type).

- In case the situation is not conducive for normal descriptive examination **a 90 minute MCQ based exam** will be conducted at the end of the Term II also.

- Marks of the Term II Examination would contribute to the final overall score.

केन्द्रीय माध्यमिक शिक्षा बोर्ड
(शिक्षा मंत्रालय, भारत सरकार के अधीन एक स्वायत संगठन)

CENTRAL BOARD OF SECONDARY EDUCATION
(An Autonomous Organisation under the Ministryof Education, Govt. of India)

Assessment / Examination as per different situations

A. In case the situation of the pandemic improves and students are able to come to schools or centres for taking the exams.

Board would conduct Term I and Term II examinations at schools/centres and the theory marks will be distributed equally between the two exams.

B. In case the situation of the pandemic forces complete closure of schools during November-December 2021, but Term II exams are held at schools or centres.

Term I MCQ based examination would be done by students online/offline from home - in this case, the weightage of this exam for the final score would be reduced, and weightage of Term II exams will be increased for declaration of final result.

C. In case the situation of the pandemic forces complete closure of schools during March-April 2022, but Term I exams are held at schools or centres.

Results would be based on the performance of students on Term I MCQ based examination and internal assessments. The weightage of marks of Term I examination conducted by the Board will be increased to provide year end results of candidates.

D. In case the situation of the pandemic forces complete closure of schools and Board conducted Term I and II exams are taken by the candidates from home in the session 2021-22.

Results would be computed on the basis of the Internal Assessment/Practical/Project Work and Theory marks of Term-I and II exams taken by the candidate from home in Class X / XII subject to the moderation or other measures to ensure validity and reliability of the assessment.

In all the above cases, data analysis of marks of students will be undertaken to ensure the integrity of internal assessments and home based exams.

Dr. Joseph Emmanuel
Director (Academics)

CHAPTER 01

Social Change and Social Order in Rural and Urban Society

In this Chapter...

Change is the only permanent and unchanging aspect of society. The discipline of sociology emerged as an effort to make sense of the rapid social change that took place in Western Europe during 17th and 19th centuries. Human civilisation has witnessed rapid and constant social change only in the last 400 years; and it has accelerated rapidly in the last 100 years.

Social Change

Social change refers to the changes that alter the "underlying structure of an object or situation over a period of time". Thus, social change include any and all changes which are big and transforming things fundamentally. Social changes are both intensive and extensive leaving a big impact over a large sector of society. Social change is a broad term, have a specific definition, therefore, various attempts have been made to understand it in terms of its causes, nature, impact and speed.

Types of Social Change

Based on its Pace or Speed

On the basis of its pace or speed, social change could be classified into the Evolutionary Changes and Revolutionary Changes.

Evolutionary Changes

Changes that take place slowly over a long period of time are called Evolutionary Change. The term evolution was given by **Charles Darwin**, a natural scientist who proposed the evolutionary theory based on the idea of survival of the fittest. According to the Darwinian theory, people change slowly or evolve by adapting to natural circumstances.

He claimed that those life forms which adopt to their environment will survive and others, who are slow or inadaptive, will die. Although Darwin's theory referred to natural processes, it soon adopted to the social world and was termed as **Social Darwinism**.

Revolutionary Changes

Changes that take place comparatively quickly or even suddenly are referred to as revolutionary change.

It is used mainly in political context, where the power structure faces to be transformation. For example, The French Revolution (1789-93) and the Soviet/Russsian Revolution of 1917. It's also used to refer sudden short and total transformations of other kind, apart from political. For example, Industrial Revolution, Telecommunications Revolution, etc.

Based on Nature or Impact

On the basis of their nature or impact, types of social changes are as follows

Structural Changes

Structural change refers to the transformation in the structure of society, its institutions and rules governing these institutions.

For example, change in the medium of currency from gold/silver to paper currency.

The introduction of paper money, made gold/silver coins obselete. This resulted in a structural change in the organisation of the financial markets and transactions. The value of money was not intrinsic or related to paper, it was representative. As a result, credit market was introduced and the structure of banking and finance also changed.

Changes in Values and Beliefs

Changes in the values and belief of people also leads to social change. For example, changes in the ideas and beliefs about childhood. Earlier, children were treated as small adults and were pushed to work and earn. However in the late 19th and early 20th centuries, a new belief regarding childhood as a special stage of life gained prominence. Now, children could not go to work and were instead supposed to get educated as child labour was banned and right to education was introduced.

Although, there are some industries in our country (such as carpet weaving, small tea shop, etc.) that even today depend basically on child labour but, child labour is illegal and employers can be punished as criminals.

Based on Causes or Sources

The most common way of classifying social change is by its causes or sources. The causes are internal (endogenous) and external (exogenous). The broad types of sources or causes of social change are discussed below

Environmental Cause/Source of Social Change

Nature, ecology and the physical environment have a significant influence on the structure and shape of society. In the past, everything, from the kind of clothes and livelihood to the pattern of social interaction was to a large extent determined by the physical and climatic conditions of their environment.

However, over time technology has transformed the role played by environment. Technology allows us to overcome and adapt to the problems posed by nature. This reduces the differences between societies living in different types of environments.

In the context of social change, environment plays an important role. Sudden and destructive events like tsunami , earthquakes, floods etc. can change societies drastically.

Environment does not only act as a destructive force, it can be a constructive source of change as well. For example, the discovery of oil in the region of West Asia or the Middle East, the discovery of gold in California, etc. had completely changed the societies of the region.

Technological and Economic Source/Cause of Social Change

Technology and economy have immensely changed the structure of the society. Technology, through its association with the economy, has caused major social changes. Various examples of these changes are as follows

- The most prominent change by technology was **Industrial Revolution**. The outcome of the Industrial Revolution was **steam engines**.
- Due to the invention of steam engines many of the handheld machines got mechanised and could run without the intervention of humans.
- Steam engine and development of various modes of transport like the steam ship and the railways transformed the economy and social geography of the world.
- After the introduction of steam engine in 1853, the trade and industry in America and Asia expanded westwards.
- **Steam ships** increased international trade and migration as it allowed faster and more reliable voyages.
- A large impact of steam power can be seen in many cases but there are also many cases in which there was a limited impact of technological invention. For example, inventions like the discovery of writing paper and gunpowder in China. However, these inventions became significant when they came under the context of modernising Western Europe. The technology of warfare was changed by gunpowder and the society was changed through the paper-print revolution.
- Technological inventions also impacted the industry in Britain. The Indian handloom industry was affected by new weaving and spinning machines along with imperial power and market forces.
- In many cases, society was also affected by some changes in economic organisations that are not related to technology. For example, the plantation agriculture of the single cash crops such as sugarcane, tea, cotton, etc created a heavy demand of labour. This resulted in the introduction of **slave trade** and **slavery** between America, Asia and Europe. This also led to forced migrations in the tea plantation of Assam.
- At present, the changes in customs duties and tariffs introduced by organisations such as World Trade Organisation can lead to prosperity of some industries and elimination of others.

Political Source/Cause of Social Change

Political forces to be one of the most important cause of social change. The most prominent example of such a change in the modern times are as follows

United States and Japan

The United States conquered Japan in Second World War after causing mass destruction with nuclear bomb. In the many years that the US ruled Japan, it brought along many changes including land reforms in Japan.

Japan tried to copy and learn from the American industry, but by 1970's, its industrial techniques, especially in the field of car manufacturing, was much ahead of the Americans. After 1970's the Japanese industrial technology dominated the world and influenced the industrial organisation of Europe and especially America. Almost every industry be it steel, automobiles, heavy engineering and even electronics were dominated by Japan.

India and Nepal

The Indian Independent movement brought a political change by ending British rule and changing Indian society. The Nepali people's rejection of monarchy in 2006 is another example of political change.

Political Change through Redistribution of Power

Political change bring about social change through the redistribution of power across different social groups and classes. For example,

The Universal Adult Franchise[1] i.e. one person, one vote principle, comprised in modern democracies. Until the introduction of democracy and voting, kings and queens claimed the rule by divine right.

When voting was first introduced, it did'nt include the whole population. Only high status social group of a particular race or ethnicity, or wealthy men with property were allowed to vote. Through long struggles, the Universal Adult Franchise was established as a norm.

The Universal Adult Franchise serves as a powerful norm that exerts pressure on every society and every government. And this norm has brought a massive social change. Although, some nations don't follow democratic norms even today; even where elections are held.

Cultural Source/Cause of Social Change

Culture is a very diversified term comprising of ideas, values, beliefs that are important to people helping them in shaping their lives. Any change in the ideas and beliefs naturally leads to changes in social life. Religion is one such domain where beliefs and norms have helped to organise the society and consequently transformed the society.

Some scholars define civilisations as the process of interaction between religion. Max Weber's work **'The Protestant Ethics and Spirit of Capitalism'** is an example of how religious beliefs and norms helps to organise society. This work highlights the role played by christian (Protestant) religious belief in establishing capital society. In Indian context, Buddhism had an impact on the social and political life of ancient India. Similarly, the Bhakti movement influenced the medival social structure including caste system.

Apart from religion, cultural values also have the power to drive economic and social change. The following examples will emphasize on the same

- Cultural change witnessed in evolution of ideas concerning the place of women in society. Women struggle for equality in the modern era have helped to change society in many ways. During World War II, women in western countries took up jobs mostly done by men. They built ships, operated heavy machinery etc., which helped them to establish equality.

- Advertising also helped in changing the role of woman in the society. Advertisement started showing women as decision makers instead of man. The economic role of women started a chain of changes with larger social impact. Therefore the advertising industry became sensitive towards the perspectives, views and representation of women.

- Games and sports are another example of role of popular culture. For instance, a cricket match often turns into a symbol of national or social pride. In India beating England at cricket carried a special meaning, especially before independence. Similarly, the world dominance of West Indies cricket team during the 1970s and 1980s was an expression of racial pride for the colonised people.

As per the above discussion, it is clear that no single factor or theory can account for social change. The causes of social change may be internal, external, accidental, deliberative and moreover, interrelated. Economic and technological cause may have cultural expressions or impact. Therefore, a social change may have many dimensions and forms.

Social Order

Social order is the tendency within the established social systems that resists and regulates change. It is the set of rules and norms that defines an order in the society . These are the norms which are consistent and gradually develop over a series of time due to evolving nature of society.

---

1 Universal Adult Franchise It gives the right to vote to all citizens, regardless of wealthy income, gender, social status, race etc.

Social order and social change are very closely related to each other. Since every society needs to prevent, discourage and control continuous change and maintain a strong and viable social system, the role of social order in this direction becomes important.

Every society strives for maintaining stability which requires that people follow the same set of rules that produce similar results and actions. Also, since most societies are divided into levels or classes based on soical status they are positioned either with respect to economic resources, political power or social status.

The powerful or dominant group resist any social change as they have a vested interest in stability. In comparison, the oppressed group support the notion of change. The 'Normal' conditions of society usually favours the rich and powerful. Therefore, social change does'nt place easily and thus, societies are generally stable.

Maintenance of Social Order

The concept of social order is not limited to just resistance to change. It refers to the active maintenance and reproduction of particular patterns of social relations and of values and norms. The maintenance of social order takes place through two means that are often used in combination for the sustenance of social order.

The two means are as follows

(*i*) **Spontaneous Abiding of Norms** Spontaneous (Natural) consent (Natural) results from shared values and norms that are accepted and internalised by people through socialisation. However, socialisation does not ensure complete obedience as people may question the present order and believe that it must be changed.

(*ii*) **Power or Coercion** In most societies, people are compelled through some form of power or coercion to ensure that institutions and individuals obey the norms. Power is defined as the ability to make other do things that you want irrespective of their wishes. If a social entity or institution is habitually in the position of power, it is dominant. Dominant forces in normal times run quite smoothly and are challenged only in special and extraordinary situations.

Role of Domination, Authority and Law in Social Order

Domination

Domination essentially refers to the power of an individual to exercise a certain degree of influence on another individual. This power of the dominant works through legitimacy which is the degree of acceptance involved in power relations.

Anything that is legitimate is considered to be proper, just and fitting, and thus is acknowledged to be a part of the social contract. In other words, a legitimate power ensures conformity to the existing norms of right, propriety (correct and acceptable moral and social behaviour) and justice.

Authority

Max Weber describes Authority as legitimate (Legal) power i.e. a power which is justified and proper. For example a judge, police officer and teacher exercises different kinds of authority. A judge, within the bounds of a courtroom, has authority; whereas on the outside he/she is like any other citizen. Similarly, a teacher has authority over the students in a classroom and this authority does'nt extend to the home of students. The power attached with an authority is exercised within a domain. And people abide by and obey authority within the proper domain.

Apart from the formalised form (i.e. judge, police officer, etc.) authority has a non-formalised form as well. For example, the authority hold by a religions leader or a criminal gang leader. A gang leader has absolute authority over people/followers without any formal specification. Similarly, as leader exercises control over his/her disciples or followers. In the same way, reputed scholars, artists, writer or other intellectual may exercise non-formalised authority in their respective fields.

Law

A law represents an explicitly clearly codified written norms or rules that every citizen in a society must follow. Law highlights the formal form of authority. In a democratic society, the legislature creates the body of laws. This law is enacted in the name of people by the people's representatives. Therefore, law forms the formal body of rules determining the governance of society.

Thus, domination works mostly through legitimate power and the codified law forms major part of this powers. But there are other kinds of power which are equally effective although they are illegitimate or not codified in law. The collective effect of legitimate, lawful and other kinds of power determines the nature and dynamics of social system.

Role Played by Contestation, Crime and Violence in Social Order

The existence of dominant, authority and law does not necessarily mean that they always meet with obedience and conformity. There are contestations or continuous disagreements as well as dissents in a society. For example, the youth rebellion wherein the youth counters cultures through their clothing, hairstyles, etc. to show their refusal to conform to prevalent norms.

Contestation refers to the dissent or protest against laws or lawful authorities. It could be expressed in the following forms

- Disagreement towards the mainstream/dominant culture given rise to 'counter culture' or youth rebellion. The refusal to conform to dominant social norms is expressed through clothing, language, lifestyle, etc. in counter virtue.
- Conventional form of contestation include elections, which are a form of political competition.
- Contestations also includes dissent/protest against laws or lawful authorities.

Contestations are part of any society, the extent to which the disagreement is tolerated is the real question. This extent is determined by the difference between legal and illegal, legitimate and the illegitimate and the acceptable and unacceptable.

Crime

A **crime** is an act that violates an existing law and going beyond the legitimate boundary of dissent defined by law. An act of crime alone cannot determine the moral worth of an act. For example, Mahatma Gandhi committed a crime by breaking the salt law at Dandi but the moral worth of this act was high. Thus, this crime of Gandhi ji was celebrated because of its moral undertone. But there are other crimes that can't claim any great moral virtue.

Violence is the extreme form of contestation that goes against the law and social norms. Violence like cirme, disrupts the social order and is an indicator of social tension and problems in society. Every act of violence is seen as being directed against the state because it has monopoly over legitimate and legal use of violence. Thus, violence highlights the failure of the regime of legitimation, consent and the open outbreak of conflicts.

Social Order and Change in Villages, Towns and Cities

Most societies in our world are divided into rural and urban sectors. Both these sectors are marked by differences in the conditions of life of the people, the forms of social organisation, the form of social order and also the kind of social change that is prevalent in the society.

Villages

Villages emerged as a result of social structural change brought by a transition from nomadic ways of life to a more settled form of life. With the development of agriculture, where people were not required to move, the social structure changed. With investment in land and technological innovations in settled form of agriculture, surplus could be produced and wealth could be accumulated. As a result, social differences came into existence and an advanced division of labour created occupational specialisations. Thus, the social organisation of a village was set-up.

Villages have a lower population density, i.e. no. of people living per unit area as they are spread out over a relatively larger area. They have a significant proportion of its population engaged in agriculture related occupations.

Town and City

Cities and Towns have a higher population density living per unit area. Majority of people are engaged in non-agricultural pursuits.

The distinction between a town and a city is more a matter of administrative concern. A town and a city are same type of settlements that differ only in terms of size. According to the census and official reports, an **urban agglomeration** comprises of a city along with its surrounding sub-urban areas and satellite settlements. A **metropolitan area** on the other hand includes a continuous urban settlement that is many times the size of a single city.

Urbanisation has been part of most countries. This process results in progressively larger portion of country's population residing in or moving to urban areas form rural settlements. Given that the developed societies are more urban and developing countries are progressively becoming urban, it is a important to note that according to the United Nations Report 2014, 54% of the world's population is already living in urban areas which will rise up to 66% by 2050. Even the Indian society also under going this process. The proportion of people living in also urban areas in India has increased from 11% in 1901 then 17% in 1951 moving to 28% in 2001 and reached 37.7 % in 2011.

Social Order and Social Change in Rural Areas

The social order and social change prevalent in villages are different because of the objectives conditions. Small size of population in villages leads to more personalised relationships. Wherein all members of a village know each other personally. Traditional pattern of society in a village leads to the dominance of caste, religion and other customary social practices. The relative power of the dominant sections is more pronounced and visible in a rural set-up.

Any form of dissent can be easily identified and punished or suppressed by the dominant forces. Also the poor have to depend much more on these dominant sections who eventually govern all the means of economic sources.

Further, villages are scattered and not very well connected to the world. As a result, all sort of social change including shift in power are very slow.

Because of the strong resilience of the social order of the villages, there exists a cultural lag between villages and towns/cities. With new modes of communication such as telephones and television as well as railroad, the existing cultural lag had reduced and the pace of change had accelerated. In addition, as villages depend on agriculture, any changes in agriculture or agrarian social relation like land reforms have a direct impact on villages.

In India, the first land reform took away lands from absentee landlords and gave them to groups who actually managed the land. These groups comprised of intermediate caste and the right over land combined with their number increased their soical status and political power.

MN Srinivas called these groups as **dominant caste,** a caste which is economically powerful and politically dominant. In many regions, dominant caste became very powerful which led them facing opposition from below or lower caste.

Similarly, Technological innovations especially in the field of agriculture also has a huge impact on rural society. Introduction of new machines impacted and altered the labour demand, cropping pattern and the economic power of different groups. Further, sudden fluctuations in agricultural prices, droughts or floods also impact the society in a negative way. In addition large scale development programmes such as the NREGA of 2005 (National Rural Employment Guarantee Act.) also started. These programmes had an enormous impact on rural people.

Social Order and Social Change in Urban Areas

Cities had always been a part of society. Before the modern era, trade, religion and war/are majorly determined the location and importance of cities. For instance old Indian cities like trading towers of Tezpur, Kozhikode etc. and temple towns of Ajmer, Varanasi or Madurai.

The modern phenomenon of urbanism is a way of life has been associated with cities. Sociologists claim that modernity and city life are closely related. Unlike villages, city is the domain of mass politics, dense populations, **group identities**[2]

and modern individual. The prevalent anonymity and amenities provide individuals with endless possibility and freedom. But, only socially and economically minority, mostly, enjoy the luxury of freedom and fulfilled life. Thus, the concentrated space squeezing in a large population intensifies identities and makes them integral in survial, resistance and assertion with respect to cities.

Problems of Urban Life

The social order in the urban regions face some major complex problems most of which is related to lack of sace. These are as follows

Spatial Problems

High population density in a city makes the urban social order focus on ensuring the spatial viability of the city. This includes ensuring housing, transportation, coexistence of residential, public and industrial areas as well as public health, sanitation, policing, public safety and monitoring the needs of urban governance. Thus, it poses many challenges of planning, implementation and maintenance which is intensified because of the stratification of the society on the basis of groups and labour.

For example, the lack of proper housing and facilities resulting in homlessness rendering people to live on streets, footpaths, slums etc. The slums comprised of homes constructed low quality material, like plastic, cardboard, etc, lacks proper civic facilities. Slums are also the place for 'dadas' or strongmen imposing their authority on people.

Communal Rivalry

The urban landscape is also a home to communal rivalry. Residential areas in cities all over the world are always Segregated by class, race, ethnicity, religion and other such variables. For example, the communal tensions between Hindus and Muslims or the **Godhra** riots in Gujarat in 2002.

Such tensions results in the conversion of mixed neighbourhoods into a single community or **ghettos**[3]. This conversion is called **ghettoisation**. Further, communal tensions also results in the creation of 'gated communities' which are essentially affluent neighbourhoods separated by walls and gates with controlled entry and exits. Such communities are separated from their surroundings and usually have their own civic facilities.

---

2 **Group Identities** Identities or groups formed on the basis of religion, race, caste, region, ethnicity and class.
3 **Ghettos** A part of a town where many people of the same race, religion etc. live in poor conditions.

Housing Patterns and Transportation

The housing patterns are linked intricately to the economy of the city. The location of residential areas relative to industrial and commercial workplaces severely affects the urban transport. If the residential areas are located at a larger distance from the industrial areas, the transport system must be created and maintained.

Transportation impacts the 'quality of life' of working people and commuting becomes a way of life. For example, the Mumbai train locals who have made many formal associations and participate in collective activities including singing bhajans, chopping vegetables, etc. Further, reliance on private road transport also creates problems of traffic congestion and vehicular pollution.

Change in Urban Areas

The question of space is central to even social change in the city. In a city, neighbourhoods and localities go through many ups and downs. The city centre or the core centre of a city has seen many changes in fortune.

The city centre had been the power centre in 19th and 20th century but it eventually went into decline in the latter half of the 20th century. Affluent classes also shift from the inner cores to the suburbs for various reasons.

Now city centre are going through a phase of revival of community life through the conversion of previously lower class into middle and upper class. This phenomenon is known as **gentrification**[4]. Various real estate developers try to effect such a conversion. However, many a times, the campaign fails and the society remains the same.

Any changes in the transportation system also affect the societies. Affordable, efficient and safe public transport shapes the social character of a city apart from influencing its economic fortunes.

---

4 Gentrification The process whereby the character of a poor urban area is changed by wealthier people moving in, improving housing and attracting new business often displacing current in habitants in the process.

Chapter Practice

Objective Questions

• Multiple Choice Questions

1. Social change refer to which of the following?
(a) A big and significant change transforming the fundamental structure of an object or situation over a period of time.
(b) A revolutionary change taking place suddenly impacting a large section of society.
(c) An evolutionary change gradually changing society over a period of time.
(d) All of the above

Ans. (d) Social change refers to a big and significant change transforming the underlying structure of an object or situation over a period of time. A revolutionary and evolutionary changes are kinds of social change. Thus, all the options are true.

2. The evolutionary theory of Charles Darwin highlights a kind of social change, which is why people in the social world often refer to the theory of Darwin as __________ .
(a) Sociological Darwinism
(b) Societal Darwinism
(c) Social Darwinism
(d) Socio-cultural Darwinism

Ans. (c) People in social world refers to Darwin's theory as Social Darwinism by employing the adaptive and evolutionary idea of this theory to the society or social world.

3. The phrase survival of the fittest implies which of the following?
(a) The survival of individuals only made possible as a group.
(b) The survival of individuals depends on their health.
(c) The survival of the individual is only possible by relying on one another.
(d) The survival of the individual is dependent on their adaptability to the environment.

Ans. (d) As per Charles Darwin, the phrase survival of the fittest highlights that the survival of the individual is dependent on their adaptability to the environment. The ones failing to do so will not survive.

4. The French Revolution and Russian Revolution represents which kind of social change?
(a) Evolutionary Change
(b) Revolutionary Change
(c) Environmental Change
(d) Contextual Change

Ans. (b) The French Revolution and Russian Revolution represents a revolutionary change. It is a kind of social change that takes place relatively quickly bringing in a drastic change in a political, technological, or structural context.

5. The Industrial Revolution, which originated in Britain, impacted societies around the globe. This revolution led to what kind(s) of social change?
(a) Technological and Economic change
(b) Economic and Revolutionary social change
(c) Revolutionary and Technological change
(d) Technological, Economical, and Revolutionary change

Ans. (d) The Industrial Revolution led to revolutionary, economical, and technological, kinds of social change.

6. The French Revolution carries a historical significance. This revolution ended up overthrowing the monarchy(or former ruling class) resulting in the peasant forces (or challengers) raising to power. This scenario highlights which of the following?
(a) A change triggered by cultural change
(b) A change triggered by economic change
(c) A change triggered by political transformation changing the governance style.
(d) A change triggered by political transformation not impacting governance.

Ans. (c) The given scenario highlights. A change triggered by political transformation without impacting governance.

7. The concept and idea of childhood as a special stage of life gained significance in the 19th and 20th centuries. Before this, children were often helping their families at work from the age of five or six, the early factory system depended on them. This realisation about childhood represents which kind of change among the following?
(a) Changes in Values   (b) Changes in the belief system
(c) Both (a) and (b)   (d) None of these

Ans. (c) The concept of childhood gaining significance as a special stage of life during the 19th and 20th centuries, highlights the changes in values and beliefs about the same. Before this shift in values and beliefs concerning childhood, children were treated as small adults who worked and earned.

8. Social order in a society is maintained with the help of which among the following?
(a) Domination and Law
(b) Law and Authority
(c) Authority, Law, and Domination
(d) Authority and Domination

Ans. (c) The social order is maintained in society as a collective impact of law, domination, and authority.

9. According to Max Weber, infusion of which factor transforms Power into Authority?
(a) Adaptability   (b) Coercion
(c) Legitimation   (d) Abolition

Ans. (c) According to Max Weber, legitimacy transformed power into authority. Authority projects the idea of just, formalised, and proper power. It also leads to acceptance devoid of coercion.

10. The leader of a sect wields _______ without it being _________ .
(a) authority, formalised   (b) power, acceptable
(c) authority, acceptable   (d) power, non-formalised

Ans. (a) The leader of a sect wields authority without it being formalised. Religions leaders, artists, intellectuals, etc, also wields the same kind of authority in their respective field.

11. A counter culture among _________ are protests against or refusal to conform to prevailing _______ .
(a) people, social norms   (b) youth, social norms
(c) people, social norms   (d) youth, social norms

Ans. (b) Counter cultures among the youth represents the refusal to conform to dominant culture and prevailing social norms.

12. Crime and violence stand in the way of social order and peace. Therefore, any act of deviance harming social order must be prevented at all costs for social harmony. Pick the correct option from this context.

(a) Violence and crime are too similar and cannot be differentiated.
(b) Crime and violence are understood in relationship with the law.
(c) The crime of breaking the salt law by Gandhiji did not carry a moral undertone.
(d) Violence does not involve physical harm like crime.

Ans. (b) Law is the reality against which crime and violence are understood. Crime represents breaking or violating the law. Violence is a crime involving physical harm, not all crime involves violence.

13. Choose the correct statement about culture.
(a) There is no cultural lag existing between the rural and urban settings and it's a myth.
(b) The culture observed in villages and cities seems to align and coincide.
(c) Culture is used as a short label for a very wide field of ideas, values, belief that are important to people.
(d) Cultural change leading to social change cannot be seen in the evolution of ideas about the peace of women in society.

Ans. (c) Option (c) is the correct answer about culture.

14. _______ defines dominant caste as _______ class.
(a) G.N. Srinivas, economically backward
(b) G.S. Ghurye, economically powerful
(c) R.K. Mukherjee, economically backward
(d) M.N. Srinivas, economically powerful

Ans. (d) M.N. Srinivas defines dominant caste as an economically powerful class in the context of a village.

15. The _______ Act was introduced in the year 2005.
(a) National Rural Employment Guarantee
(b) National Sports University
(c) National Employment
(d) National Rural and Urban Guarantee

Ans. (a) The National Rural Employment Guarantee Act was introduced in the year 2005.

• Assertion-Reasoning MCQs

Direction (Q. Nos. 1-4) *Each of these questions contains two statements, Assertion (A) and Reason (R). Each of these questions also has four alternative choices, any one of which is the correct answer. You have to select one of the codes (a), (b), (c) and (d) given below.*

Codes
(a) Both A and R are true and R is the correct explanation of A
(b) Both A and R are true but R is not the correct explanation of A
(c) A is true, but R is false
(d) A is false, but R is true

1. Assertion (A) Socialisation helps in the practice, understanding, and internalisation of norms, values, and beliefs in society.

Reason (R) Social stability and social order is the sole result of socialisation.

Ans. (c) Although socialisation helps in the practice, understanding and internalisation of norms, values, and beliefs in society but it's not the sole reason determining the same. Social order cannot be a reality without domination, authority and law. Thus, A is true and R is false.

2. Assertion (A) Counter culture is popular among the youth in society informing their way of living.

Reason (R) The refusal to conform to dominant social norms gives rise to counter culture.

Ans. (c) The counter-culture is popular among the youth as it expresses the youth culture where they exhibit reluctance to accept, follow, or conform to the dominant culture or social norms prevalent in society. Therefore, Both A and R are true and R is the correct explanation of A.

3. Assertion (A) Social order helps to maintain peace and stability in society.

Reason (R) The dominant group or class in society wants to preserve the social order as it serves their interest.

Ans. (c) Social order helps to maintain peace and stability in society. But this idea of social order has different meanings to different groups of people in society. The dominant group/class in society wants to preserve the social order as it works in their favour, whereas the minority or suppressed group wished to change the same. Hence, the statement R is not a correct explanation of A.

4. Assertion (A) Power is defined as the ability to make others do what you want regardless of what they want.

Reason (R) When a social entity is habitually in the position of power its said to be dominant.

Ans. (d) Power is the ability to make others do what you want regardless of what they desire. Domination is established when a social entity (a person, institution or group) habitually or routinely stays in the position of power. Thus, both A and R are true, R is not the correct explanation of A.

• Case Based Questions

1. Read the following passage and answer the following questions accordingly.

Religious beliefs and norms have helped organise society and it is hardly surprising that changes in these beliefs have helped transform society. So important has religion been, that some scholars have tended to define civilisations in religious terms and to see history as the process of interaction between religions. However, as with other important factors of social change, religion too is contextual — it is able to produce effects in some contexts but not in others. Max Weber's study 'The Protestant Ethic and the Spirit of Capitalism' showed how the religious beliefs of some Christian Protestant sects helped to establish the capitalist social system.

(i) The ability of religion to transform society has led some scholars to interpret _______ in term of _______ interactions.

(a) civilisations, religious   (b) civilisations, harmonic

(c) civilisations, religious   (d) civilisations, symbolic

Ans. (a) The ability of religion to transform society has led some scholars to interpret civilisations in term of religious interactions. The changes witnesses in religious beliefs have resulted in societal transformation. This ability of religion has led scholars to describe civilisation in terms of religious interactions.

(ii) In the protestant Ethics and Spirit of capitalism, Max Weber claimed _______ Christians helped to establish capitalist society.

(a) Catholic   (b) Protestant

(c) Orthodox   (d) Latin Catholic

Ans. (b) In the protestant Ethics and Spirit of capitalism, Max Weber claimed Protestant Christians helped to establish capitalist society.

(iii) What does the phrase religion is too contextual in the given passage imply?

(a) Religion always results in social change irrespective of other factors.

(b) Religion only when coupled with other factors will result in social change.

(c) Religion, without any additional factors, produces social change.

(d) The success of social change determines by religious forces is context-bound.

Ans. (d) In the background of the given passage, religion may necessarily lead to social change. It mean the success of societal transformation informed by religion is context-bound, i.e., it works in some situations and does'nt work in some.

2. Read the following passage carefully and answer the following questions accordingly.

Across the world, the city centre – or the core area of the original city – has had many changes of fortune. After being the power centre of the city in the 19th and early 20th century, the city centre went through a period of decline in the latter half of the 20th century. This was also the period of the growth of suburbs as the affluent classes deserted the inner city for the suburbs for a variety of reasons.

City centres are experiencing a revival now in many major western cities as attempts to regenerate community life and the arts bear fruit. A related phenomenon is of gentrification.

(i) Within the structure of a city, where does the heart of the city lie?
  (a) Malls   (b) Cinema Halls
  (c) Both (a) and (b)   (d) City centre

Ans. (d) It is the city centre where the heart of the city lies within the structure of a city. In other words, the city centre represents the core of the original city. Malls and cinema halls are common facilities available in every city.

(ii) The growth of suburbs accentuated as a result of the decline of city centres and the _________ class deserted the _______ to live in suburbs.
  (a) affluent, city   (b) middle, city
  (c) wealthy, inner city   (d) upper-middle, city

Ans. (c) The growth of suburbs accentuated as a result of the decline of city centres and the wealthy class deserted the inner city to live in suburbs.

(iii) The process of transforming low income neighbourhood into middle/high income neighbourhood is known as
  (a) Spatial problem
  (b) Communal rivalry
  (c) Domination
  (d) Gentrification

Ans. (d) The process of transforming low-income neighbourhood into middle/high-income neighbourhood is known as gentrification.

PART 2
Subjective Questions

• Short Answer (SA) Type Questions

1. Define social change and mention its types.

Ans. Social change refers to the change in the system in which human social relationship remains organised, controlled and stable. It is a universal phenomenon wherein only the rate of change varies.

Social change is significantly a very complex and broad term. Therefore, it has been often defined in terms of its types. Social changes has been characterised into various types depending on different basis. They are as follows

  (i) On the basis of pace
    • Evolutionary change
    • Revolutionary change
  (ii) On the basis of impact
    • Structural change
    • Change in values and beliefs
  (iii) On the basis of cause/source
    • Environmental change
    • Technology and economy change
    • Political change
    • Cultural change

2. Write a short note on Social Darwinism?

Ans. The term 'Social Darwinism' emerged with the concept of evolutionary changes that was proposed by Charles Darwin. Darwin stated that evolution refers to changes that take place slowly over a long period of time. He used evolution to propose how living organism evolve over time by adapting to their environment. He proposed the idea of 'survival of the fittest'.

According to the Darwinian theory, only those survive who are best adapted to their situations and those who do not or are slow die in the long run. Although, this theory referred to natural process, it was understood in sociological process giving way to the concept of Social Darwinism.

3. What are some of the significant social changes that have taken place in the Indian society?

Ans. Indian society is characterised by a significant number of social changes. Some of them are as follows
  • Caste system that was prevalent in the Indian society has now come to an end. Thus, the eradication of caste system has taken place.
  • The institution of child marriage has also been recognised as illegal in the Indian society.
  • There has been a marked shift from joint family system to nuclear family system.
  • Status of women has been improving over the years along with dowry system becoming irrelevant in the Indian society.

4. Would you agree with the statement that rapid social change is a comparatively new phenomenon in human history? Give reasons for your answer.   **(NCERT)**

Ans. Yes, the statement that rapid social change is a comparatively new phenomenon in human history is correct. Human beings have existed on planet earth for approximately five lakh years, but they have had a civilised existence for only about 6000 years out of which we have seen constant and rapid changes in the last 400 year and this has been accelerated in last 100 years.

The rapid change is a collective impact of social, political, cultural and economic changes. The French Revolution, Industrial Revolution, technological advancements urbanisation etc. triggered social, political and economical changes across the globe. Introduction of democracy transformed the political structure and governance. All these changes points to the modern society and thus its safe to say social change is a modern or new phenomena in human history.

5. How is social change to be distinguished from other kinds of change?   **(NCERT)**

Ans. Social change is a general term that refers to almost any kind of change that is not qualified by some other terms, such as economic or political change. However, it does not mean that it includes any and all kinds of changes. Social changes are changes which transform things fundamentally or which significantly alters the underlying structure of an object or situation over a period of time.

Social change is broad and complex term. It has many dimensions determining its nature, impact, magnitude, pace, etc. Social change causes big impact to a larger section of society intensively and extensively. The impact of a social change could be a collection of political, economic, cultural, or even structural change. These features of social change distinguishes it from other kinds of change.

6. What do you understand by structural change? Explain with examples other than those in the text.
      (NCERT)

Ans. **Structural Change** It refers to transformations in the structure of society. It is generally with reference to rules on the basis of which certain types of institutions operate and function. The changes that actually happen in the prevailing institutions of society is referred to as structural change.

The emergence of paper money as a medium of currency brought a significant structural change in organisation of financial market and transaction. Paper money made gold/silver coins obselete, but it also introduced the idea of money used as tool facilitating exchange of goods and services without itself being instrinsically valuable, unlike gold/silver coins. The notion that anything representing value (i.e. inspiring trust) could be used as money. And this laid the foundation for credit market determining the structural change in banking and finance. The economic life was recognised with the advent of paper money.

7. Describe some kinds of environment related social changes.   **(NCERT)**

Ans. Nature, ecology and physical environment always had a significant influence on the structure and share of society.

This was particularly true in the past when human beings were unable to control or overcome the effects of nature.

For instance, people living in desert were unable to practice settled agriculture. Their food, clothing, livelihood and even social interactions were determined by physical and climatic conditions of their environment.

Similarly, sudden catastrophic events such as earthquake, volcanic eruptions, flood or tidal waves etc. also lead to social change. For instance the tsunami of 2004 drastically impacted the societies of Indonesia, Sri Lanka, Andaman Islands and parts of Tamil Nadu. These changes are permanent and irreversible in nature.

Environmental factors could also result in constructive change. For instance, the discovery of oil in the Middle East and discovery of gold in California completely changed these societies for gold.

8. 'Technological changes do not always ensure a significant impact'. Justify.

Ans. Technology is one of the driving cause for effective social changes. The industrial revolution drastically transformed the industries and economy accross the globe by introducing machine technology. Steam engine is one such invention improving the modes of transport facilitating trade and enabling large-scale production. Although, in some cases technology does'nt seen to cause a significant impact. For instance, the discovery of gunpowder by China, had only limited impact until it was introduced in the modern context of warefare. The circumstances supporting the use of gunpowder emerged hater and it ended up transforming the technology of war fare. Similarly, the inovation in the textile industry in Britain, ended up destroying the handloom industry of India, when it (Britain) became the imperial power and controlled the market situation.

Therefore, it is Justifiable to say that technological change do not always ensure a significant impact.

9. What is authority and how is it related to domination and the law?

Ans. Max Weber has defined authority as legitimate power considered to be justified or proper. Authority in society is based upon economic factors.

In other words, an individual assumes authority because of his/her official job description which gives a certain legitimate power. For example, a judge authority works in court, outside court, he is under the authority of a police man.

Relation of Authority with Domination and Law

Domination works through legitimate power or authority/a major portion of which constitutes the law. Similarly/law is a system of rules through which human behaviours are controlled and regulated. Without authority, law cannot be formed and implemented and without law authority is not normalised.

10. Contestation, crime and violence are always present in a social order. Elaborate.

Ans. The existence of dominant authority does not necessarily mean that thay always muel with obedience and conformity.

People can have different opinions even if they follow the same law. Hence, there always a scope for dissent. The following statements will elaborate on the same

- Contestations or continuous disagreement and dissents are always present in society. Societies allow dissent but only to a certain extent. If the limit is exceeded, it becomes a crime which allows for a reaction, usually, from the law enforcing agencies.
- The notion of crime is derived from law. It represents an act that violates in existing law or goes beyond the boundary of legitimate dissent.
- Closely related to the idea of crime is violence, which is the extreme form of contestation going beyond the law as well as social norms. It's a product of social tension challenging the authority of the state.
- The state can punish an individual for any act of violence, as it has monopoly over the legitimate and legal use of violence. Apart from self defence, all the other acts of violences, are thus, considered directed against the state becoming a crime.

11. Why is village called a social unit?

Ans. A village is called a social unit as sociological analysis revealed the presence of a different social order in the social set up of village.

A village comprises of few people living over a larger scattered region. The village people depend on agriculture and agricultural allied activities for their livelihood. As a result, do they not only share the same traditional customs and beliefs but are found in a more personalised relationships.

People live in peace and harmony resulting in cohesion among them. The cooperative social relationship among the residents of village justify it as a social unit.

12. "Community feeling is there in rural community". Explain the statement.

Ans. It is true that community feeling is there in rural community. Mutual relations among rural people are based on cooperation because of which community feeling exists among them.

All the village members are ready to help each other in the time of crisis. Unity exists among them due to direct and informal contact. They collectively face their problem and take part in sorrow and happiness all together.

Unlike the isolated and formal social relationships and social interaction witnessed in urban areas or cities, villages form a cohesive unit. The cohesiveness is based on the shared culture, where people share their worries, problem, social situation, mode of labour etc. Especially the lower population density with people spreaded across a larger area makes this community feeling even stronger. Everyone knows and identifies with one another. In urban getting the heterogeneity and high population density makes it difficult to generate a community feeling, in the fast paced city life.

• Long Answer (LA) Type Questions

1. Discuss some of the factors behind social change in the society.

Ans. Social change happens due to a variety of reasons ranging from physical factors, biological factors, demographic, cultural and technological factors. These factors are discussed as follows

(i) **Physical Factors** Human's life gets impacted by the environmental conditions; changes experienced in the climatic and physical environmental conditions alters the surrounding and determines human life. In habital geographical conditions are preferred by people as they find the conditions livable.

(ii) **Demographic Factors** Population density is one of the key of demographic factures causing social change. high population density results in problems related to space/housing, in adequate resources to meet the need, communal rivalry and transpiration issues.

(iii) **Factor Related to Technology** Technological factors are significant part of material culture. Before technology, societies functioned differently. The technological advancements in communication, transport and machines have changed the society drastically. The large-scale production is possible with machines. It reorganised the labours and brought significant social changes impacting the social order.

2. What are some kinds of changes brought about by technology and the economy?   (**NCERT**)

Ans. The changes brought by technology and the economy are as follows

- Technology and economy have revolutionised the way society has progressed over the years. Since the year 1750, many technological machines were invented that led to the advent of Industrial Revolution.
- Production in industries started growing rapidly on a large scale that not only empowered man to control certain aspects of nature but also his economic condition.
- Dams were constructed to control the fury of floods. The introduction of steam engines allowed easy migration and transportation which in turn allowed industrialisation. Thus, social structure started transforming.
- Globalisation slowly transformed the world into one single economic village.

- Division of labour and specialisation of labour became the new norm of modern societies. However, such changes in the pattern of technology also brought certain negative things along. Labours were replaced by machines and unemployment rose in the society. In this manner the social changes were brought about by technology and economy.

3. How are a village, town and a city distinguished from each other?

Ans. **Villages** Villages are a unit of the rural community, where rural life upholds itself and does perform its functions. It is simple community spread out or scattered over a relatively larger area.

It has a lower density of population most of whom are engaged in agriculture linked occupations.

A village is often characterised by personalised relationships where every member knows every other member of a society. However, such a set up is not well connected to the world because of which social changes are slow and gradual.

Town/Cities Cities and towns have a higher density of people living per unit area. Majority of people living in town or cities are engaged in non-agricultural pursuits. Cities and towns are generally characterised by industrialisation and urbanisation where they have become commercial hubs.

As a result, the life of an individual is complex and multidimensional such that social changes are quick and drastic.

Town and cities differ only on administrative basis. A town and a city are some sorts of settlements that differ only in terms of size.

4. What is meant by social order and how is it maintained? **(NCERT)**

Ans. **Social Order** It refers to the way that the various components of society-social structures and institutions, social relations such as social interaction and behaviour, and cultural aspects like norms, beliefs, and values-work together to maintain the existing state of affairs.

Social change acquires meaning against the backdrop of continuity or lack of change. Since social order essentially resists change, it also has a tendency to be attached to social customs which are connected to social systems.

In other words, social order is not just resistance to change, also the active maintenance and reproduction of particular pattern of social relations and of values and norms.

Ways of Maintaining Social Order

There are two ways of maintaining social order which are as follows

(i) First is when people spontaneously want to abide by a set of rules and norms. The shared values and norms are accepted and internalised by people through socialisation.

(ii) Second is when people are compelled through some form of power or coercion to ensure that institutions and individuals obey the norms. If any individual or organisation challenges the dominant order, they are suppressed or punished.

5. What are some features of social order in rural areas? **(NCERT)**

Ans. Rural areas which are quite distinct from the urban areas have some very peculiar features of social order that are summarised as follows

- **Agriculture the Sole Occupation** Major occupation of the rural area is dominated by agriculture and allied activities. Land is the prime asset of a rural society upon which the entire economic system and development of people as well as villages rests.

- **Simplicity in Living** People residing in rural areas lead a very simple lifestyle. People residing in rural areas do not aspire much in terms of living conditions.

- **Less Population and Homogeneity** Population size of rural areas is very small compared to urban areas. People have common traditional customs and rituals resulting in increased homogeneity in their cultures. Also there is no significant difference in the income level of the people in the rural areas.

- **Strong Resilience** The relative power of the dominant sections is more pronounced in a rural set up. They govern the economic sources, thus making the social order resilient to change. All kinds of dissent is easily identified, suppressed and punished.

- **Impact of Innovation** As the rural society is dependent on the agrarian mode of livelihood, all agricultural technological innovations have a great impact on the social order of rural areas.

6. What are some of the challenges to social order in urban areas? **(NCERT)**

Ans. The social order in the urban regions face some major complex problems most of which is related to a lack of space. Some problems are discussed as follows

- **Spatial Problems** High population density in a city makes the urban social order focus on ensuring the spatial viability of the city. This includes ensuring housing, transportation, coexistence of residential, public and industrial areas as well as public health, sanitation, policing, public safety and monitoring the needs of urban governance. Thus, it poses many challenges of planning, implementation and maintenance which are intensified because of the stratification of the society on the basis of groups and labour.

- **Communal Rivalry** The urban landscape is also a home to communal rivalry that results from segregation prevalent in the residential areas of the society. For example, the communal tensions between Hindus and Muslims or the Godhra riots in Gujarat in 2002.

- **Housing Patterns and Transportation** The housing patterns are linked intricately to the economy of the city. The location of residential areas relative to industrial and commercial workplaces severely affects the urban transport. If the residential areas are located at a larger distance from the industrial areas, the transport system must be created and maintained. Transportation impacts the quality of life of working people and commuting becomes a way of life. Further, reliance on private road transport also creates problems of traffic congestion and vehicular pollution.

7. Read the following passage and answer the question that follow.

For obvious reasons changes associated with agriculture or with agrarian social relations have a very major impact on rural societies. Thus, measures like land reform which alter the structure of land ownership have an immediate impact. In India, the first phase of land reforms after independence took away proprietary rights from absentee landlords and gave them to the groups that were actually managing the land and its cultivation in the village. Most of these groups belonged to intermediate castes, and though they were often not themselves the cultivators, they acquired rights over land. In combination with their number, this factor increased their social status and political power, because their votes mattered for winning elections. M.N. Srinivas has named these groups as the 'dominant castes'.

Define Dominant caste. What are the changes that have taken place in rural households due to agriculture?

Ans. Dominant castes is a term given by M.N. Srinivas to those people who belonged to intermediate castes but slowly uplifted their status by acquiring the rights over land and thus political power. This led to a caste division in rural societies that affected the social status of people.

There are some changes taken place in rural house holds due to agriculture. These are as follows
Agriculture has transformed the structure of land ownership in rural societies. The prevalence of absentee landlords was mitigated by land reforms post-independence.

- The ownership of the lands was given to people who were actually managing the land and its cultivation.
- M.N. Srinivas called the new emerging class as dominant class. In many regional contexts, the dominant caste grew economically dominating the electoral politics and thereby the countryside.
- In recent years, these dominant castes have face assertive uprisings form the lower castes and most backward castes. Many states, including Andhra Pradesh Bihar, Uttar Pradesh, and Tamil Nadu, have experienced significant social upheavals as a result of this.

8. Read the following passage and answer the question that follow.

Changes in values and beliefs can also lead to social change. For example, changes in the ideas and beliefs about children and childhood have brought about very important kinds of social change, there was a time when children were simply considered small adults — there was no special concept of childhood as such, with its associated notions of what was right or wrong for children to do. As late as the 19th century for example, it was considered good and proper that children start to work as soon as they were able to. Children were often helping their families at work from the age of five or six; the early factory system depended on the labour of children. It was during the 19th and early 20th centuries that ideas about childhood as a special stage of life gained influence.

It then became unthinkable for small children to be at work, and many countries passed laws banning child labour. At the same time, there emerged ideas about compulsory education, and children were supposed to be in school rather than at work, and many laws were passed for this as well. Although there are some industries in our country that even today depend on child labour at least partially (such as carpet weaving, small tea shops or restaurants, matchstick making and so on), child labour is illegal and employers can be punished as criminals.

What change happened during the 19th and 20th centuries? How can change in values and beliefs lead to social change?

Ans. In the 19th and 20th centuries, ideas about childhood as a very special stage of life to gain. It was impossible to see a small child working and many countries passed laws banning child labour. There were also ideas about compulsory education that gained prominence and popularity.

- Changes in values and beliefs can lead to social change as changes in ideas about things changes the mind of an individual. The notion about children has for example, changed over the years as earlier. Children were treated as small adults and they would start working at an early age with their family. Slowly, the concept of childhood evolved and it's believed that children should be educated till a certain age before they are pushed to work. For example, banning child labour and implementing compulsory education. However, the most common method of categorising social change is by its causes or origins. Internal (or endogenous) and external (or exogenous) causes are often pre-classified. Environmental, technological, economic, political, and cultural change are the five broad forms of influences or causes of social change.

9. Explain the differences between rural and urban societies in detail.

Ans. Rural and urban societies have following distinctive features are as follows

Differentiating Factors	Rural Society	Urban Society
Family Set-up	Rural families have complete control over its members. Joint family system is prevalent here, where agricultural occupation unifies the family members with equal participation.	In contrast, family has very less control and influence over its members. Nuclear families are more prevalent in urban societies.
Marriage	Marriage in rural societies carry a religious undertone and it performed by the elders of family with all the traditional rituals.	Marriage takes the form of a contract which could be broken any time and it becomes a mattter of personal choice. In contrast to rural areas, here inter-caste marriages are quite common.
Occupation	Agriculture is the primary occupation and the entire family is dependent on the same for survival.	In comparison, urban socieities have diverse occupational choices and job opportunities.
Population Density	Rural areas are sparsely populated exhibiting to low population density.	In contrast, urban areas have high population density giving rise to the problems like overpopulation. It increases the competition for resources.
Women's Status	In rural settings a woman's status is very low. Women experiences less freedom in decision making. Her roles are restricted to caretaker of family and children.	In comparison women in urban areas are educated and economically independent. The exercise independent decision-making and in general enjoy a much higher status.

• Case Based Questions

1. Interpret the pictures given below and answer questions 1-3 accordingly.

Picture 1.1

Picture 1.2

(i) Picture 1.1 represents the girl looking after her sibling in a rural village. In comparison to picture 1.2, what does this girl seems to be lacking, childhood or education?

Ans. The girl in picture 1.1 seems to be lacking the opportunity to attain education and her childhood compared to picture 1.2. The girl in picture 1.1 who is taking care of her sibling is being treated as a small adult.

(ii) Which picture shows the change witnessed in the condition of women or girls over the years? Does this change highlight a cultural change?

Ans. Picture 1.2 shows the change witnessed in the condition of women or girls. The opportunity for education is the deciding factor for this change. Yes, this change highlights cultural change and improvement in the scenario of women or girls.

(iii) "Social structure in villages tends to follow a traditional pattern". Which picture justifies this statement and why?

Ans. Picture 1.1 justifies the statement mentioned in the question. Because a girl taking care of her sibling supports the traditional social practices, where a girl is not provided the mandatory education and helps in house chores.

2. Interpret the image (a) given below and answer the questions accordingly.

Image (a) A commercial centre in a city

(i) In comparison with the image (a), define the notion of a rural region or village and the factors differentiating both?

Ans. In comparison with image (a), a village represents a population settlement based on a particular form of social organisation. The population density and economic activities are factors differentiating villages and city centers. Villages have lower population density where the economy is dominated by agriculture.

(ii) What is the difference between the city depicted in image (a) and metropolitan areas?

Ans. A metropolitan area is different from a city, as it includes more than one city, or a continuous urban settlement many times the size of a single city.

(iii) Define the phenomenon that has led to the increase in the population density in a city.

Ans. Urbanisation is the phenomenon that has led to the increase in the population density of a city. Urbanisation represents the phenomenon of people migrating to urban regions or cities from rural areas.

3. Read the following passage carefully and answer the questions.

Given the small population, it is also very difficult to gather large numbers, particularly since efforts towards this connot be hidden from the powerful and are very quickly suppressed. The relative power of the dominant sections is much more because they control most avenues of employment and most resources of all kinds. So, the poor have to depend on the dominant sections since there are no alternative sources of employment or support. Given the small population, it is also very difficult to gather large numbers, particularly since efforts towards this cannot be hidden from the powerful and are very quickly suppressed.

(i) The passage mentioned above points a clear picture of the conditions in urban settings. Is this statement true or false? If true/false, why?

Ans. This statement is false because the passage talks about the conditions of a rural/village setting. The small population and the dependency of the poor on dominant sections due to no alternatives show the reality of a village setting.

(ii) In the background of the passage, what is the nature of social order in villages? And why?

Ans. The nature of social order is strong and resilient in villages. Because there is a strong power structure already in place and change in the sense of power shifts are slow and late to arrive in rural areas compared to urban regions.

(iii) How did M.N. Srinivas define the dominant caste in a village?

Ans. According to M.N. Srinivas, a dominant caste is an economically powerful section or group of people in a village and thus they dominate the electoral politics of a village.

4. Read the following passage carefully and answer the questions.

Another way of looking at the relationship between social change and social order is to think about the possible reasons why society needs to prevent, discourage, or at least control change. In order to establish itself as a strong and viable social system, every society must be able to reproduce itself over time and maintain its stability. Stability requires that things continue more or less as they are— that people continue to follow the same rules, that similar actions produce similar results, and more generally, that individuals and institutions behave in a fairly predictable manner. Most societies most of the time are stratified in unequal ways, that is, the different strata are differently positioned with respect to command over economic resources, social status, and political power.

(i) The idea of a society reproducing itself over time represents which associated concept? Identify the concept and define the same.

Ans. The idea of society reproducing itself is associated with the concept of social order. Social order refers to the active maintenance and reproduction of a particular pattern of social relations, values and norms.

(ii) The different strata are differently positioned with respect to command over economic resources, social status, and political power. What are the two common strata or groups prevalent in any society? Which among these groups are economically and politically strong?

Ans. Every society has a ruling or dominant group and an oppressed or subordinate group. The dominant or ruling group in a society is economically and politically strong and powerful compared to the subordinate group.

(iii) Identify and define the opposing concept in relation to the notion of social order?

Ans. The concept of social change is an opposing concept to the notion of social order. Social change refers to the change experienced in the underlying structure of an object or situation over a period of time.

5. Read the following passage carefully and answer questions.

In the old ways of writing and recounting history, the actions of kings and queens seemed to be the most important forces of social change. But as we know now, kings and queens were the representatives of larger political, social and economic trends. Individuals may indeed have had roles to play, but they were part of a larger context. When one society waged war on another and conquered or was conquered, social change was usually an immediate consequence. Sometimes, conquerors brought the seeds of change and planted them wherever they went. At other times, the conquered were actually successful in planting seeds of change among the conquerors and transformed their societies.

Although there are many such examples in history, it is interesting to consider a modern instance — that of the United States and Japan.

(i) The "social change" mentioned in the given passage represents which kind of social change? Identify and define the same.

Ans. The social change mentioned in the given passage represents a political social change. A political social change represents a change in the political organisation or structure of a society.

(ii) "The modern instance of the United States and Japan". Identify this instance. What does this instance historically significant?

Ans. The modern instance in the above statement represents the famous war between the United States and Japan during the II World War, when the former emerged victorious. This victory or war carries historical significance because the United States used nuclear bomb to secure this victory where the world witnessed mass destruction unlike the one seen before.

(iii) "In the old ways of writing and recounting history, the actions of kings and queens seemed to be the most important forces of social change". Does this statement represent monarchy or democracy,

Ans. The statement mentioned above represents monarchy, where kings and queens seemed to be the most important source of social change as they governed or ruled over the people. In comparison, democracy is system where people have the liberty to vote for their representative.

Chapter Test

Multiple Choice Questions

1. The new spinning and weaving machines destroyed the .... industry of the Indian subcontinent with technological innovations in the textile industry in Britain.
   (a) transport
   (b) handloom
   (c) silk
   (d) cotton

2. Most modern societies must also depend on .... to ensure that institutions and individuals conform to established social norms.
   (a) Power Coercion
   (b) Coercion
   (c) Both (a) and (b)
   (d) None of these

3. .... refers to a standard or conventional forms of contestation.
   (a) Elections
   (b) Competition
   (c) Conflict
   (d) None of these

4. .... is the one of the defining features of the modern state.
   (a) Monopoly over legitimate use of violence within and beyond its jurisdiction.
   (b) Monopoly over legitimate use of violence within its jurisdiction
   (c) Monopoly over legitimate use of violence beyond its jurisdiction
   (d) None of the above

Short Answer Type Questions

5. What is structural change? Give an example.
6. What do you understand by power?
7. What is the meaning of the term socialisation?
8. Define authority as given by Max Weber.
9. "Universal Adult Franchise brought about a major political change". Justify
10. Discuss briefly the technological factor responsible for social change.
11. Explain how social order is maintained?

Long Answer Type Questions

12. Explain the various types of changes which are seen in urban society?
13. The concept of social order is interlinked with the concepts of domination authority, law, contestation, crime and violence. Elaborate.
14. Social change in the context of a village is a slow and late at arrival relative to the urban setting. Justify the same by elaborating the reasons behind it.
15. City represents the domain of a modern man enjoying enormous freedom and opportunities. Is this notion of freedom and opportunity being applicable to all the individuals in city? Comment.

Answers

1. (b) *2.* (d) *3.* (a) *4.* (b)

CHAPTER 02

Introducing Western Sociologists

In this Chapter...

- Context of Sociology
- Karl Marx's Vision of Society
- Durkheim's Vision of Sociology
- Max Weber's Vision of Society

Sociology evolved in the 19th century in Western Europe after the revolutionary changes, which changed the living conditions of the people. Ideas of **Karl Marx**, **Emile Durkheim** and **Max Weber** laid the foundations of sociology as a subject and their ideas and insights have been relevant even today.

Context of Sociology

There were three major revolutions responsible for the development of sociology in Europe. These were

(i) The Enlightenment or dawning of the age of reason (Scientific revolution)

(ii) The French Revolution

(iii) The Industrial Revolutions

These revolutions played an important role in the development of sociology as a discipline. These are discussed as follows

Enlightenment of Western Europe

The late period of 17th and 18th centuries saw new radical ways of thinking about the world. This was referred to as Enlightenment. It is the ability to think rationally and critically. During this period, people who could think were considered as a complete humans whereas those who could not think and had lack of knowledge were considered as not fully evolved humans. They were considered natives of primitive societies. Society became answerable to rational analysis and comprehensible to other humans.

Thus, enlightenment helped in development of attitudes of mind. In present time, it is referred to as **secular**, **scientific** and **humanistic**.

French Revolution

The French Revolution started in 1789 and introduced the political **sovereignty**[1] at the level of individuals and nation-states.

Due to the declaration of Human Rights, questioning legitimacy of privileges inherited by birth was made possible. It also indicated upliftment of the individual from the oppressive rule of the religious and **feudal**[2] **institutions** that dominated France before the revolution.

Serfdom (system of bonded labour) and **Serfs** (bonded labourers earlier peasants) had been tied to landed estates which were owned by the members of the aristocracy. The taxes paid by the peasants to the **feudal lords** were cancelled.

Citizens were free and enjoyed equality before the law. The state had to protect the privacy of the autonomous individuals, and state laws could not intervene the domestic or private life of people.

---

1 **Sovereignty** Sovereignty is the supreme authority within a territory sovereignty entails hierarchy within the state, as well as external autonomy for states.

2 **Feudal System** It was the combination of the legal, economic, military and cultural customs that flourished in medieval Europe between the 9th and 15th centuries.

A separation was built between the public and private households. Religion and family became more **private** and education became more **public**.

The **nation-state** was redefined as a sovereign entity with a centralised government. The ideals of the French Revolution-**liberty**, **equality** and **fraternity** became the basis of the modern world.

Industrial Revolution

Industrial Revolution laid the foundations of modern industry in the world. It started around the late 18th and early 19th centuries in Britain. The modern industry has two aspects. They are as follows

(*i*) Growth of science and technology and its systematic application to industrial production, with the invention of new types of machines and harnessing of new sources of power.

(*ii*) New ways of organising labour and markets on a large scale that promoted mass manufacturing of goods.

New machines and new methods of obtaining power facilitated the production process and gave rise to the **factory system** and **mass manufacture of goods**.

For example, **Spinning Jenny**[3] and various versions of the steam engine facilitated the production process in the following manners

- Goods were manufactured on a large scale for markets around the world. The raw materials used in production were imported from different nations. Thus, Industrial Revolution established large-scale industry as a worldwide phenomenon.

- Many workers had to work in factories and this led to children, men and women undertaking hazardous occupations for long hours and lower wages.

- Cities and towns became prominent and dominant forms of human settlement because a large number of rural people especially men, migrated to urban areas in search of work in big factories.

- The urban areas became small and densely populated as it catered to the housing of large diverse rural migrants. The rich and powerful occupied the cities but working class lived in slums.

- New kinds of states with modern types of governance emerged. Facilities like health, sanitation, crime control and general development created the demand for new kinds of knowledge.

From the sociological viewpoint, industrial revolution can be understood as

- Sociological thought was associated with the scientific analysis of development in industrial society. Due to this, observers argued that sociology was the science of the new industrial society.

- The modern industrial society made it easier or possible to generate **empirical**[4] information regarding the trends in **social behaviour**[5].

- The scientific information generated by the state of monitor and maintained the health of its social body became the basis for reflection on society. Sociological theory was the result of this self-reflection.

Karl Marx's Vision of Society

Karl Marx was a German philosopher. Marx was basically a social thinker who wanted to end oppression and exploitation. He advocated scientific socialism and total destruction of capitalism.

Marx had a view that a society progresses through different stages. These stages were **primitive communism**, **slavery**, **feudalism** and **capitalism**. Capitalism was the latest phase of human advancement, but Marx believed that it would give way to socialism.

Levels of Alienation in Capitalist Society

According to Marx, Capitalist society was marked by an intensifying process of **alienation**[6] operating at following three levels

(*i*) Humans aliented from the nature.

(*ii*) Humans are alienated from each other and or fellow individuals. Capitalism results in a unique form of social organisation, where the workers are individualised as they are involved in minimal or no interaction with their fellow workers. This alienates workers from one another and their relationship becomes market oriented.

(*iii*) Working people alienated from i.e. the profit or gains achieved us a result of hardwork as they do not have any control over their work and products. It is decided by the owners of the means of production.

Finally, as an effect of all these levels of alienations, human beings are also alienated from themselves. They struggle to make their lives meaningful in a system where they are both more free and more alienated and less in control of their lives than before.

---

3 **Spinning Jenny** It was invented by James Hargreaves. It is a multi-spindle spinning frame.
4 **Empirical** Knowledge based on observations, research or experiment instead of ideas.
5 **Social Behaviour** The process of communication/interaction taking place among the people in a society.
6 **Alienation** A process in capitalist society by which human beings are separated and distanced from (or made strangers to) nature, other human beings, their work and its product.

Capitalism and Society

Marx believed that capitalism is a necessary and progressive stage of human history. It created the precondition for an **egalitarian** future i.e., free from exploitation and poverty.

Marx believed that slowly capitalism would be transformed, by the working class of a society through a revolution and lead to a socialistic society. Marx undertook an elaborate study of political, social and economic aspects of society to understand the working of capitalism.

Productive Forces and Production Relations

Marx's conception of the economy was based on the concept of a mode of production. He kept modes of production (primitive communism, slavery, feudalism and capitalism) as a base that included the **productive forces** and **production relations**.

Productive forces refer to all the means or factors of production. e.g. land, labour, technology, sources of energy, electricity, coal, petroleum, etc. Production relations refer to all the economic relationships and forms of labour organisations involved in production. Production relations are also property relations or relationships based on the ownership or control of the means of production. For example, in the mode of production i.e. the primitive communism, the productive forces consisted mostly of nature like forests, land, animals and so on. It also includes basic forms of technology like simple stone tools and hunting weapons.

Production relations were based on community property and included tribal forms of hunting or gathering which were the prevalent forms of labour organisation. The economic base thus, consisted of productive forces and relations of production. All the social, cultural and political institutions of society were based on the economic base. Thus, the institutions like religion, art, law, literature or different forms of beliefs and ideas became part of the **superstructure** which was built on top of the base.

Economic System and Economic Structures

Marx argued that people's ideas and beliefs originated from the economic system to which they belonged.

Marx laid great emphasis on economic structures as he believed that they formed the foundations of every social system throughout human history. If we understand how the economy works and how it has been changing in the past, we can learn how to change society in the future. This change can be brought through class struggle.

Class Struggle and Conflict

According to Marx, the people should be classified on the basis of **production process** instead of religion, language, nationality, etc. People occupying the same social position in the production process, modes of production and property relations are identified as a class. As per Marx, classes are formed through a historical process of class struggle, where the conditions and forces of production created conflict among the existing classes in society.

With the change in mode of production i.e. the production technology and the social relations of production, conflicts between different classes arises. It ultimately leads to struggle. For example, the capitalist mode of production creates the working class, which is a new urban, property-less group created by the destruction of the feudal agricultural system.

Marx points out that serfs[7] (Agriculture workers) and small peasants were deprived of their earlier sources of livelihood when their lands were taken away. This led to establishment of a new social group of property-less people who were forced to work under the capitalist class in urban areas/cities (who were also the owners of the factories). They struggled in cities to adjust themselves.

Class Struggle : As a Major Source for Change in Society

Marx was a strong believer in the concept of class struggle and believed it to be the main source for changes in the society. In *The Communist Manifesto*, Marx and Engels presented their views. They further advocated that the history of class struggle varied in different historical era. As society evolved from the primitive to the modern through distinct phases, each characterised by particular kinds of conflict between the oppressor and oppressed classes.

The major opposing classes of each stage were identified from the contradictions of the production process. Like in capitalism, the **bourgeoisie** (capitalist) class owned all the means of production such as factories and machines, land, capital, etc. In comparison, the working class lost all the means of production (land) which they owned in the past. Thus, in the capitalist social system, workers had no choice but to sell their labour for wages in order to survive because they had nothing else.

Conflicts and Revolution

Conflicts do not occur automatically. For conflicts, a class needs to be aware or conscious of its class interests and identities. Without the development of **class consciousness** and identification of the rivals class interest and identities, class conflict cannot occur.

---

7 **Serfs** They are peasants under feudalism, specifically relating to manorialism. Serfdom was a condition of bondage, which developed primarily during the High Middle Ages in Europe and lasted until the mid-19th century.

When dominant class is overthrown by the previously dominated or sub-ordinated classes, it is termed as **revolution**. In Marx's theory, economic processes created contradictions which generated class conflict.

The result of such conflict is the overthrow of a dominant ruling class. But economic processes did not automatically lead to revolution, social and political processes were also needed to bring about a total transformation of society.

The presence of ideology is one reason why the relationship between economic and socio-political processes become complicated. In every epoch,the ruling classes promote a dominant ideology. This dominant ideology or way of seeing the world, tends to justify the domination of the ruling class and the existing social order.

For example, dominant ideologies may encourage poor people to believe that they are poor not because they are exploited by the rich but because of 'fate' or because of bad deeds in a previous life and so on. However, dominant ideologies are not always successful and they can also be challenged by alternative world views or rivals ideologies.

As consciousness spread unevenly among classes, how a class will act in a particular historical situation cannot be pre-determined. Hence, according to Marx, economic processes generally tend to generate class conflicts, though this also depends on political and social conditions. The favourable conditions in class conflicts lead to revolutions.

Durkheim's Vision of Sociology

Emile Durkheim is regarded as the founder of sociology as a formal discipline. He was the first professor of sociology in Paris (1913), who argued that society was a **social fact**[8] which existed as a **moral community** over and above the individual. In his book **The Elementary Forms of Religious Life**, Durkheim attempted to develop a secular understanding of religion.

The ties that bound people in groups were essential for the existence of a society. These ties or social solidarities exerted pressure on individuals to conform to the norms and expectations of the group. This constrained individual's behaviour pattern, limiting variation within a small range.

Constriction (i.e., narrowing) or less availability of choice in social action means that social behaviour could be predicted as these behaviours followed a pattern. Thus, by observing patterns of behaviour one could identify the norms, codes, and social solidarities ruling/governing individuals.

Thus, the existence of otherwise 'invisible' things like ideas, norms, values and so on could be empirically verified by studying the patterns of social behaviour of people as they related to each other in a society.

For Durkheim, the society was to be found in the codes of conduct imposed on individuals by collective agreement. It was evident in the practices of everyday life. The scientific understanding of society that Durkheim sought to develop was based on the recognition of moral facts. For him moral facts are phenomena like others consisting of rules of action that are recognisable by certain distinctive characteristics. Then, it must then be possible to observe them, describe them, classify them and look for certain laws explaining them.

He emphasised greatly on moral facts that were manifestations of particular social conditions. The morality appropriate for one society was inappropriate for another. For Durkheim, the prevailing social conditions could be deduced from the moral codes. This made sociology similar to the natural sciences. As Durkheim had an objective to establishing sociology as a rigorous scientific discipline.

Features of Sociology

Durkheim considered sociology as a new scientific discipline from the point of view of two important features. They are as follows

Subject Matter of Sociology

According to Durkheim the subject matter of sociology i.e. the study of social facts was different from other sciences. Sociology, according to him, focuses on the **emergent level**, i.e., the level dealing with complex collective social phenomenon.

The social institutions (i.e. religion, family, etc) or social values (i.e., friendship, patriotism, etc.) represents a complex whole or collective body which are different from or larger than its constituent parts. For example, a family is a social institution formed by family or individuals. Therefore according to Durkheim, the aim of focusing on the emergent level in Durkheim's view was to gain a general understanding of the institution of the family, not the individuals comprising the same.

Although the collectives like social bodies, social institutions etc. are comprised entirely of individuals but these collectives have more significant meaning than the involved individuals.

Thus, social entities like teams, political parties, street gangs, religious communities, nations etc, were on a higher level than the level of individuals. This is the emergent level that sociology primarily focus upon.

---

8 Social Fact Aspects of social reality that are related to collective patterns of behaviour and beliefs, which are not created by individuals but exert pressure on them and influence their behaviour.

Sociology as an Empirical Discipline

Sociology is also an empirical (experimental) discipline, like most of the natural sciences (i.e., physics, chemistry, biology, etc.) This was a difficult claim to make by Durkheim as social phenomenon is abstract in nature. We cannot see a Jain community, or a Nepalese speaking community in the same way we can see a tree or a cloud.

Even in the case of a social institution like a family, one can only directly see the individual members who make up the collective body (family); we cannot see the collective but body itself. But Durkheim claimed and demonstrated through his work that sociology is an empirical discipline that could study and analyse these abstract concepts through observation and research.

Concept of Social Fact

For Durkheim, society is a social fact which existed as a moral community over and above the individual.

Although social facts are not directly observable, they could be indirectly observed through the patterns of social behaviour. **Suicide** is one such study of Durkheim where he used empirical data to study the social fact of suicide.

In his study of suicide, Durkheim observed how the case of suicide of each individual was specific to the circumstances of individuals. The average rate of suicide aggregated across the individual in a community was a social fact. In other words, Durkheim concluded that suicide was a social fact, which could be studied indirectly through the social behaviours of individuals in a community.

According to Durkheim, social facts are like things that are external to individuals but constraining their behaviour at the same time. Institutions like law, education and religion constituted a social fact that represent a collective, originating from the association of people.

Social facts are general in nature, as they are applicable to an entire society independent of the individuals such as beliefs, values, or collective practices.

Division of Labour in Society

In his first book, *Division of Labour* Durkheim demonstrated the method of analysis to explain the **evolution of society** from primitive to the modern. He classified a society by the nature of social solidarity which existed in that society. He illustrated this with his concepts of mechanical and organic solidarity.

According to him, primitive society was based on mechanical solidarity while the modern society was based on organic solidarity.

As per Durkheim mechanical solidarity had the following features

- It was found in societies with a small population with similarities among the individual members.
- This solidarity was based on similarity and personal relationships where a collection of self-sufficient groups of people was engaged in similar activities or functions. Societies with mechanical solidarity were not tolerant of differences and any violation of norms of the community and were met with harsh punishments.
- Mechanical solidarity based societies have repressive laws designed to prevent deviation from community norms. This was because the individual and the community were so tightly integrated that it was feared that any violation of codes of conduct could result in the disintegration of the community.

Organic solidarity was prevalent in modern societies based on the heterogenity of its members. It's found in large societies with impersonal and independent social relationships. Such a society is based on institutions, and each of its constituent groups or units is not self-sufficient but dependent on other units/groups for their survival. Interdependence is the essence of **organic solidarity**. It celebrates individuals and allows for their need to be different from each other and recognises their multiple roles and organic ties.

Collective Consciousness

The laws that exist in the modern society are **restitutive** while in a traditional society laws are **repressive** in nature. This means that in modern societies, the law aims to repair or correct the wrong that is done by a Criminal Act. By contrast, in primitive societies the law sought to punish wrong doers and enforced a sort of collective revenge for their acts. In modern society, the individual was given some autonomy, whereas in **primitive societies** the individual was totally submerged in the collectivity.

A characteristic feature of modern society is that individuals with similar goals come together voluntarily to form groups and associations. As these groups have different goals, they remain distinct from each other and do not seek to take over the entire life of its members. Thus, individuals have many different identities in different contexts.

This enables individuals to emerge from the shadow of the community and establish their distinct identity in terms of the functions they perform and the roles they play.

Since, all individuals have to depend on others for the fulfilment of their basic needs like food, clothing, shelter and education, their intensity of interaction with others increases. Impersonal rules and regulations are required to govern social relations in such societies because personalised relations can no longer be maintained in a large population.

> ### Emile Durkheim
>
> Emile Durkheim was born on 15th April, 1858 in Epinal in the Lorraine region of France. He was from an Orthodox Jewish family. His father and great grandfathers were Jewish priests or **rabbis**. Emile too was initially sent to a school for training rabbis.
>
> **Timeline of Events in the Life of Emile Durkheim**
>
> 1876:   He entered the Ecole Normale Superieure in Paris to study philosophy.
>
> 1887:   He was appointed lecturer in social sciences and education at the University of Bordeaux.
>
> 1893:   He published Division of Labour in Society, his doctoral dissertation.
>
> 1895:   He published Rules of Sociological Method.
>
> 1897:   He founded Anee Sociologique,the first social science journal in France; and publishes his famous study, suicide.
>
> 1902:   He joined the University of Paris as the Chair of Education. Later, in 1913 the chair was renamed Education and Sociology.
>
> 1912:   He published The Elementary Forms of the Religious Life.
>
> 1917:   He died at the age of 59, heartbroken by the death of his son, Andre in World War I.

Max Weber's Vision of Sociology

Max Weber was a leading German social thinker, who wrote extensively on many subjects and focused on developing an interpretive sociology of social action, power and domination. Another major concern of Weber was the process of rationalisation in modern society and the relationship of the various religions of the world with this process.

Max Weber and Interpretive Sociology

Weber argued that the overall objective of the social sciences was to develop an 'interpretive understanding of social action' and social sciences were very different from the natural sciences which aimed to discover the objective 'laws of nature' governing the physical world.

Since, the central concern of the social sciences was with social action and since human actions necessarily involved subjective meanings, the methods of enquiry of social science also had to be different from the methods of natural science. For Weber, 'Social action' included all human behaviour that was meaningful, that is, action to which actors attached a meaning.

In studying social action, the sociologist's task was to recover the meanings attributed by the actor. To accomplish this task the sociologist had to put themselves in the actor's place and imagine what these meanings were or could have been.

Sociology was thus, a systematic form of **empathetic understanding**, that is, an understanding based not on 'feeling for' (sympathy) but 'feeling with' (empathy). The empathic (or empathetic) understanding which sociologists derive from this exercise enables them to access the subjective meanings and motivations of social actors.

Weber was among the first to discuss the special and complex kind of 'objectivity' that the social sciences had to cultivate. The social world was founded on subjective human meanings, values, feelings, prejudices, ideals and so on. In studying this world, the social sciences inevitably had to deal with these subjective meanings.

In order to capture, these meanings and describe them accurately, social scientists had to constantly practise 'empathetic understanding' by putting themselves (imaginatively) in the place of the people whose actions they were studying. But this investigation had to be done objectively even though it was concerned with subjective matters.

Empathetic and Ideal Type Understanding

For empathetic understanding, Weber believed that sociologist should practice **value neutrality.** Value neutrality refers to the duty and responsibility of the social researcher to overcome his personal biases while conducting any research.

It means the 'empathetic understanding' required the sociologist to faithfully record the subjective meanings and motivations of social actors without allowing his/her own personal beliefs and opinions to influence this process in any way.

Weber recognised that this was very difficult to do because social scientists were also members of society and always had their own subjective beliefs and prejudices. However, they had to practise great self-discipline, exercise an 'iron will', in order to remain 'value neutral' when describing the values and worldviews of others.

Concept of Ideal Type

Weber suggested another methodological tool known as the **ideal** type to gain sociological understanding. It represented a logical model of a social phenomenon comprising its most significant characteristics.

Ideal types exaggerate some features of phenomenon that are considered to be analytically important and ignore or downplay others.

Ideal type should correspond to reality in a broad sense, but its main job is to assist analysis by bringing out important features and connections of the social phenomenon being studied. An ideal type is to be judged by how helpful it is for analysis and understanding, not by how accurate or detailed a description it provides.

Uses of Ideal Type

It was used to analyse the relationship between the ethics of world religions and the rationalisation of the social world in different civilisations. Through this ideal type, Weber described three types of authorities-**traditional**, **charismatic** and **rational-legal**. The traditional form of authority was one that began with old customs and traditions. While charismatic was derived from the divine sources or the 'gift of grace', the rational-legal was based on legal demarcation of authority. Rational-legal authority which prevailed in modern times was epitomised in the bureaucracy.

Bureaucracy

It is a type of mode of organisation where behaviour in the public domain is regulated by strict bureaucracy rules and regulations. As a public institution, restricts the power of the officials in regard to their responsibilities and did not provide absolute power to them.

Bureaucratic authority is characterised by following features

- **Functioning of Officials** Within the bureaucracy, officials have fixed areas of **official jurisdiction**[9] governed by rules, laws and administrative regulations. The regular activities of the bureaucratic organisation are distributed in a fixed way as official duties. Moreover, commands are issued by higher authorities for implementation by subordinates in a stable way, but the responsibilities of officials are strictly delimited by the authority available to them.

  As duties are to be fulfilled on a regular basis, only those who have the requisite qualifications to perform them are employed. Official positions in a bureaucracy are of independent nature and they continue beyond the duration of any occupant.

- **Hierarchical Ordering of Positions** Authority and **office**[10] are generally placed on a graded hierarchy where the higher officials supervise the lower ones. This allows scope of appeal to a higher official in case of dissatisfaction with the decisions of lower officials.

- **Reliance on Written Document** Management of a **bureaucratic organisation** is carried out on the basis of written documents which are preserved as records. These documents are also a part of the public domain which is separate from the private life of the officials.
- **Office Management** As it is a specialised and modern activity, it requires trained and skilled personnel to conduct operations.
- **Conduct in Office** Official's conduct in office is governed by exhaustive rules and regulations that are usually pre-decided by the government. These separate his/her public conduct from his/her behaviour in the private domain. Also since, these rules and regulations have legal recognition, officials can be held accountable.

Weber argued that individual requires high-level skills and specialisations, as it forms the basis of modern society. The legal boundation on officials prevented them from exercising unlimited power and made them accountable to their clients. Because the work was carried out in the public domain.

Max Weber (1864-1920)

Max Weber was born on 21st April, 1864 in Erfurt, Germany into a Prussian family. His father was a magistrate and a politician who was follower of Bismarck.

Timeline of Events in the Life of Max Weber

1882:	He went to Heidelberg to study law.
1884:	He studied at the Universities of Gottingen and Berlin.
1889:	He submitted his doctoral dissertation on 'A Contribution to the History of Medieval Business Organisations'.
1891:	He submitted his habilitation thesis (entitling him to be a teacher) on Roman Agrarian History and the Significance for Public and Private Law.
1894-96:	He was appointed as a Professor of Economics first at Freiburg and then Heidelberg.
1903:	He became the Associate Editor of the Journal Archives for Social Science and Social Welfare.
1904:	He travelled to the USA and published The Protestant Ethic and the Spirit of Capitalism.
1918:	He took up a specially created chair in Sociology at Vienna.
1919:	He was appointed as a Professor of Economics at the University of Munich.
1920:	Weber died. His major works were translated and published as book after his death. These include The Protestant Ethic and the Spirit of Capitalism (1930), From Max Weber: Essays in Sociology (1946), Max Weber on the Methodology of the Social Sciences (1949), The Religion of India (1958) and Economy and Society (3 volumes, 1968).

---

9 **Official Jurisdiction** It is the legal term for the authority granted to a legal entity to enact justice.

10 **Office** In the context of bureaucracy, office is a public post or position of impersonal and formal authority with specified powers and responsibilities.

Chapter Practice

Objective Questions

• **Multiple Choice Questions**

1. The emergence of sociology is a result of which among the following?
(a) The French Revolution   (b) The Enlightenment
(c) The Industrial Revolution (d) All of these

Ans. (d) The emergence of sociology was a collective impact of the Enlightenment, the French Revolution and the Industrial Revolution. Thus (d) is the correct answer.

2. The enlightenment is also known as _____ .
(a) the age of rationality   (b) the age of criticality
(c) the age of reason   (d) the age of revolution

Ans. (c) The enlightenment is also known as the age of reason because it promoted a new way of thinking emphasising rational thought as the central feature of human beings.

3. The _____ Revolution advocated the arrival of _____.
(a) Industrial, political sovereignty
(b) French, political sovereignty
(c) Industrial, human rights
(d) Industrial, freedom

Ans. (b) The French Revolution advocated the arrival of political sovereignty.

4. What were the ideals of the French Revolution?
(a) Liberty, sovereignty and equality
(b) Liberty, fraternity and sovereignty
(c) Equality, sovereignty and liberty
(d) Equality, liberty and fraternity

Ans. (d) Equality, liberty and fraternity were the ideals of French Revolution.

5. The ideas put forward by the French Revolution resulted in a new understanding concerning the separation between the _____ of state and _____ realm of the household.
(a) private realm, public   (b) private realm, private
(c) public realm, public   (d) public realm, private

Ans. (d) The French Revolution put forward ideas resulting in a new understanding concerning the separation between the public realm of state and private realm of household.

6. The Industrial Revolution gave rise to _____ and _____ of goods.
(a) the factory system, mass production
(b) the caste system, minimal production
(c) the factory system, production
(d) the caste system, mass production

Ans. (a) The Industrial Revolution gave rise to the factory system and mass production of goods.

7. _____ and _____ became the dominant form of human settlements as a result of Industrial Revolution.
(a) Villages and towns   (b) Factories and towns
(c) Cities and towns   (d) None of these

Ans. (c) Cities and towns became the dominant form of human settlements as a result of Industrial revolution.

8. Which of the following statement is not true about Industrial Revolution.
(a) The Industrial Revolution was began in Britain in 18th and early 19th centuries.
(b) The application of science and technology to the industrial process, especially the invention of new machines was a huge part of the Industrial Revolution.
(c) The Industrial Revolution did impact the ways of organising labour to a large extent.
(d) All of the above

Ans. (c) The Industrial Revolution had two major aspects. One was the application of science and technology in the industrial process and the second was the evolution of new ways of organising labour and market on a large scale. Thus, option (c) is not true about Industrial Revolution.

9. As per Karl Marx, which are the stages through which the human society has progressed?
(a) Primitive, communism, slavery and capitalism
(b) Slavery and Feudalism
(c) Both of the above
(d) None of the above

Ans. (c) Karl Marx argued that human society has progressed through different stages namely, primitive, communism, slavery, feudalism and capitalism.

10. According to Karl Marx, which stage of society would lead the way to socialism?
(a) Slavery   (b) Capitalism
(c) Feudalism   (d) Communism

Ans. (b) Karl Marx stated that capitalism was the latest phase of human development which would give way to socialism.

11. Which of the following statements is not true about Durkheim?
(a) Durkheim was born on 15th April, 1858 in Epinal.
(b) Durkheim was the first to become a professor of Sociology.
(c) Durkheim believed that class struggle was the major driving force for change in any society.
(d) Durkheim also stated that society is a study of social facts.

Ans. (c) It was Marx, not Durkheim who believed that class struggle was the major driving force for change in any society. Thus, option (c) incorrect about Durkheim.

12. Sociology concerned itself exclusively with what he called the 'emergent' level. The most famous example of his use of a new kind of empirical data is in his study of Suicide. Who is he in this context?
(a) Max Weber   (b) Emile Durkheim
(c) Karl Marx   (d) None of these

Ans. (b) It was Emile Durkheim who stated that sociology concerns itself with the emergent level. In his famous study of Suicide, Durkheim presented an empirical study of social facts.

13. In every epoch, the ruling classes promote a dominant ideology. This dominant ideology, the way of seeing the world, tends to justify the domination of the ruling class and the existing social order. What term does Marx use for the ruling/dominant class in modern capitalist society?
(a) The dominant group   (b) The bourgeoisie
(c) The proletariat   (d) Both (b) and (c)

Ans. (b) In the modern capitalist society, as per Karl Marx, the bourgeoisie or the capitalists are the dominant class as they owned all the means of production.

14. Marx and Engels presented their views in a clear and concise manner in their work. Its opening lines declare, 'The history of all hitherto existing societies is the history of class struggle'? Which is this work?
(a) The Division of Labour
(b) The Elementary Forms of Religion
(c) The Communist Manifesto
(d) Economy and Society

Ans. (c) Marx and Engels in their infamous work 'The Communist Manifesto' shared their view on class struggle and stated that the history of all hitherto existing societies is the history of class struggle.

15. Sociology dealt with the scientific analysis of development in industrial society. Thus, sociology came to be known as _______.
(a) the discipline of new industrial society
(b) the science of new society
(c) the discipline of a new society
(d) the science of new industrial society

Ans. (d) Sociology came to be known as the science of new industrial society as it dealt with the scientific analysis of the development taking place in the industrial society.

• Assertion-Reasoning MCQs

Directions (Q. Nos. 1-4) *Each of these questions contains two statements, Assertion (A) and Reason (R). Each of these question also has four alternative choices, any one of which is the correct answer. You have to select one of the codes (a), (b), (c) and (d) given below.*

Codes
(a) Both A and R are true and R is the correct explanation of A
(b) Both A and R are true, but R is not the correct explanation of A
(c) A is true, but R is false
(d) A is false, but R is true

1. Assertion (A) Capitalist society was marked by an ever-intensifying process of alienation operation at different levels.

Reason (R) In a capitalist society, human beings are alienated from nature, each other, fruits of labour, and finally from themselves.

Ans. (a) Both (A) and (R) are true and (R) is the correct explanation of A. Karl Marx argued that capitalist society is marked by the process of alienation experienced at different levels. In a capitalist society, human beings are alienated from nature, each other, the product of labour, and ultimately from themselves (or their true nature). Therefore, Both (A) and (R) are correct and (R) explains (A) correctly.

2. Assertion (A) In primitive society, the nature of law is repressive.

Reason (R) In primitive society, the individual and the community were so tightly integrated that it was feared that any violation of codes of conduct could result in the disintegration of the community.

Ans. (a) Both (A) and (R) are true and (R) is the correct explanation of (A). In primitive tightly, the law is repressive in nature as individuals are tightly integrated into society. Due to this any violation is seen as a threat against the community and was met with repressive punishments. Therefore, Both (A) and (R) are correct and (R) explains (A) correctly.

3. Assertion (A) The laws of modern society are 'restitutive' in nature rather than 'repressive'.

Reason (R) Mechanical solidarity characterises modern society and is based on the heterogeneity of its members.

Ans. (c) (A) is true, but (R) is false. Emile Durkheim stated that modern society has restitutive law, unlike the repressive laws of traditional society. He also stated that modern society is held together based on organic solidarity (not mechanical solidarity) informed by the heterogony of its members. Thus, Assertion (A) is true and but Reason (R) is false.

4. Assertion (A) Sociology was a systematic form of 'empathetic understanding', that is, an understanding based not on 'feeling for' (sympathy) but 'feeling with' (empathy).

Reason (R) Weber was among the first to discuss the special and complex kind of objectivity that the social sciences had to cultivate.

Ans. (b) Both (A) and (R) are true, but (R) is not the correct explanation of (A). Weber was the proponent of interpretive sociology which was based on the systematic form of empathetic understanding of social action. He was also the first one to discuss the complex and special kind of objectivity in social sciences. Thus, Both Assertion (A) and Reason (R) are correct, but (R) is not the correct explanation of A.

• Case Based MCQs

1. Read the following passage carefully and answer the questions.

The changes in the production system also resulted in major changes in social life. The factories set up in urban areas were manned by workers who were uprooted from the rural areas and came to the cities in search of work. Low wages at the factory meant that men, women and even children had to work long hours in hazardous circumstances to eke out a living. Modern industry enabled the urban to dominate over the rural.

Cities and towns became the dominant forms of human settlement, housing large and unequal populations in small, densely populated urban areas. The rich and powerful lived in the cities, but so did the working classes who lived in slums amidst poverty and squalor.

(i) Which among the following is responsible for "the changes in production system"?
(a) The French Revolution
(b) The Industrial Revolution
(c) The Enlightenment
(d) All of the above

Ans. (b) Industrial Revolution is responsible for the changes in production system.

(ii) "The factories set up in urban areas were manned by workers who were uprooted from the rural areas and came to the cities in search of work."
What does the movement of the workers in this statement imply?
(a) The process of Industrialisation
(b) The process of Migration
(c) Both (a) and (b)
(d) The process of Urbanisation

Ans. (d) The movement of workers (i.e., workers uprooted from the rural areas and came to cities) reflects the process of urbanisation. This process results in people's movement/migration from rural areas to cities in search of jobs among other reasons.

(iii) The rich and the powerful lived in the cities whereas the __________ ended up living in __________ .
(a) working class, slums   (b) ruling class, slums,
(c) working class, villages   (d) ruling class, villages

Ans. (a) The rich and the powerful lived in the cities whereas the working class ended up living in slums.

2. Read the following passage and answer the questions.

He classified a society by the nature of social solidarity which existed in that society. Mechanical solidarity is founded on the similarity of its individual members and is found in societies with small population. It typically involves a collection of different self-sufficient groups where each person within a particular group is engaged in similar activities or functions. As the solidarity or ties between people are based on similarity and personal relationships, such societies are not very tolerant of differences and any violation of the norms of the community attracts harsh punishment.

This was because the individual and the communities were so tightly integrated that it was feared that any violation of codes of conduct could result in the disintegration of the community. His effort to create a new scientific discipline with a distinct subject which can be empirically validated is clearly manifested in the way he discusses the different types of social solidarity as social facts. His objective and secular analysis of the social ties which underlie different types of society laid the foundation of sociology as the new science of society.

(i) Who is "He" in the above passage?
  (a) Emil Durkheiem (b) Emile Durkheim
  (c) Emilie Durkheim (d) Emilye Dukheime

Ans. (b) He is Emile Durkheim in the given passage.

(ii) Mechanical solidarity is found in which society?
  (a) Primitive society (b) Modern society
  (c) Both of these (d) None of these

Ans. (a) Mechanical solidarity is a characteristic feature of a primitive society, which is comprised of a small population where the people are involved in similar activities or functions.

(iii) "Such societies are not very tolerant of differences and any violation of the norms of the community attracts harsh punishment." What does harsh punishment imply?
  (a) The law in such societies is restitutive in nature.
  (b) The law in such societies is repressive in nature.
  (c) Both of the above depending on the scenario or violation.
  (d) None of the above

Ans. (b) The term 'harsh punishment' in the statement mentioned above implies that law in such societies, i.e., primitive societies, are repressive in nature. An act of difference or violation is seen as a threat to the integrity of the community.

PART 2
Subjective Questions

• Short Answer (SA) Type Questions

1. How was Industrial Revolution responsible for giving rise to sociology? **(NCERT)**

Ans. The Industrial Revolution brought many changes in the society. The invention of new machines led to evolution in the organisation of labour and markets. The factory system and manufacturing on mass scale led to changes in modes of production around the world.

The growth of industries, urban space, slums and modern form of government was a social consequence of these developments. As a result, the Industrial Revolution caused significant changes in society, which ultimately gave rise to the concept of sociology. The scientific analysis of development and study of social behaviour in industrialised societies were the main subjects of sociology. This was made possible by empirical observation and study of the information about social indicators generated by the state.

2. Explain class struggle theory of Karl Marx.

Ans. Karl Marx developed his theory of class struggle in his analysis of the capitalist society. Karl Marx was of the view that human society has passed through different stages of development *viz* primitive, communal, ancient, feudal and capitalist. Each of these stages has been defined by a mode of production. The factors of production are in the hands of the oppressors and they control them while the oppressed are completely devoid of them.

There always exists a conflict between the haves and the have nots. Also when the proletariat class becomes conscious and slowly acquires revolutionary character the bourgeoisie is overthrown out of power.

3. What are the various components of a mode of production? **(NCERT)**

Ans. Karl Marx's philosophy of capitalism was based on the notion of modes of production which was associated with the historical period.

The various modes of production at a general level are primitive, communism, slavery, feudalism and capitalism.

At a general level, the mode of production defines the way of life specific to an era. At a specific level, the mode of production is determined by the economic base comprising productive forces and production relations. Productive forces include all the means of production, whereas production relations include the economic relationships and ways in which labour is organised.

4. Distinguish between sub-structure and superstructure.

Ans. The differences between sub-structure and superstructure are as follows

Sub-structure	Superstructure
It is the lower part of the society.	It is the upper part of the society.
It forms the base of the society and includes labourers, production means, experience of production, production relations.	It includes different aspects of social life such as political, intellectual, legal, cultural, etc.
It forms economic structure of the society.	It forms social structure of the society.
The base or sub-structure is pre-dominant in society.	The superstructure often affects the base or sub-structure.

5. Explain the concept of class antagonism given by Karl Marx.

Ans. Karl Marx gave the concept of class antagonism which actually means class struggle. Marx wrote history of all the existing societies and observed the history of class struggle. He said that antagonism exists between two classes e.g. the oppressor who exploits and the oppressed who becomes the victim in the hands of the oppressor.

He used the terms for these two classes as Bourgeoisie and the Proletariat class. The Bourgeoisie were the oppressor who owned all the means of production i.e. capital, existing factories, machinery, land, etc.

The Proletariat is the one who is oppressed and has no means of production. They have no access to resources but basically forms a part of labour in the society.

6. Discuss Durkheim's notion of social solidarity.

Ans. Durkheim had the view that in every society there are some values, ideas, beliefs, ways of behaviour, institutions and laws which bind the society into a single unit. Since, these common elements are present in a society, the relations and the unity or solidarity exists in the society. These elements eventually increase acceptance and solidarity in society.

This is the type of solidarity often referred to as social solidarity. If these essential elements start to disintegrate then the society gradually breaks up into many parts. Hence, social solidarity provides a society with a social base of functioning.

7. What are social facts? How do we recognise them? **(NCERT)**

Ans. **Meaning of Social Facts** According to Emile Durkheim, sociology is the study of social facts. Social facts are things that are external to an individual and constrain their behaviour. They are general in nature. They represent the collective social behaviours of people.

Social institutions like law, education and religion also constitute social facts along with beliefs, feelings and collective practices.

Recognition of Social Facts

In order to prove that sociology is based on social facts, Durkheim carried out the study on 'suicide'. According to it, suicide is a personal choice that an individual commits, but the average rate of suicide in society reflects social behaviour thus making it a social fact. Hence, social facts can be recognised through social behaviour and the aggregate patterns of social behaviour.

8. The laws of modern society are 'restitutive' in nature rather than 'repressive'. What does Durkheim mean by this statement?

Ans. Durkheim had the view that crimes are an integral part of the society and modern society has laws to deal with those crimes. In traditional societies, laws were made to punish the criminals for their wrongful act. They were repressed and kept in subordination and were revenged for their act. However in modern societies, the law aims to repair or correct the wrong that is done by a criminal act. Also the individual has been given some autonomy in the modern society. This was completely absent in traditional and primitive societies.

9. What is the difference between 'mechanical' and 'organic' solidarity? **(NCERT)**

Ans. The differences between mechanical and organic solidarity are as follows

Mechanical Solidarity	Organic Solidarity
It is majorly found in primitive societies.	It is found in modern societies.
It is found in those societies that have less population.	It is found in societies that have a large population and greater impersonal relationships.
It is basically a group of people who are self-sufficient in their own ways and are engaged in similar type of activities.	The people in this group are not self-sufficient but are dependent on other groups for their survival.
This type of society is not very tolerant of differences and violent.	This type of society is tolerant and is independent of each other.
It has repressive laws that prevent deviation or opposition from the norms of the community.	It has components of restitutive law, which means that it tries to correct the wrong done by the criminals in the society.

10. Explain the characteristics that define collective representation.

Ans. A collective representation is defined by the following characteristics

(i) Social facts are the collective representations. The language of the community and the monetary system of the nation are its examples.

(ii) It is the subject matter into which the ideas of the society have been condensed.

(iii) The collective representations reflect collective values and beliefs. Types of popular myths, religious doctrines and the customs and traditions are all helpful in understanding collective representations.

(iv) Collective representations express the way in which the objects are affected by the social value.

(v) The basic social life is difficult to explain using only the psychological factors. The individuals who follow the societal values have collectively established the ways of thinking and behaving in the society. It is something that is not created by one individual alone but is a result of collective thinking.

11. Explain the three ideal types of domination.

Ans. Weber has identified three ideal types of domination or authority. These are as follows

    (i) **Rational Legal Domination** It is based on rational legitimacy and rests on the belief that there are some kinds of legality in the norms. It even accepts the rights of those who exercise authority under legally defined rules to issue commands.

    (ii) **Traditional Authority** Traditional authority is based on traditional legitimacy and it is based on habitual way of thinking. The source of traditional authority was custom and precedence meaning that whatever established from the past and has formed a norm will constitute traditional form of authority. In short, in traditional authority the ability and right to rule is passed down, often through heredity. It does not change overtime, does not facilitate social change, tends to be irrational and inconsistent.

    (iii) **Charismatic Domination** This type of domination is based on charismatic legitimacy. Charisma essentially means a type of gift or grace and Charismatic legitimacy depends upon the devotion to the specific and exceptional sanctity, heroism or exemplary character of an individual. Charismatic domination is something which is based on the normative patterns that are prescribed by the individuals possessing charisma.

12. Try to find out what Marx and Weber wrote about India. **(NCERT)**

Ans. **Karl Marx** He referred to the villages of India as 'little communities'. He had opinion that India was a self-sufficient group which had no contact with the outside world. India had its own institutions and beliefs that controlled the human behaviour.

Marx also opposed the British rule in Indian society and was totally against it. He wrote many articles on India under the British Raj, in order to throw light upon his views.

Max Weber He studied India under his works on the 'Sociology of Religion'. Weber understood the Indian society as orthodox and suppressed, under the barriers of the caste system. Throughout his studies, he emphasised the need of the traditional household in an Indian society and also wrote about the position of women in the Indian society.

13. According to Weber, what is the overall objective of social sciences?

Ans. Weber argued that the overall objective of the social sciences was to develop an 'interpretive understanding of social action'. He believed that these sciences were very different from the natural sciences, which aimed to discover the objective 'laws of nature' governing the physical world. His view was that the methods of enquiry of social science also had to be different from the methods of natural science. 'Social action' included all human behaviour that was meaningful, i.e, action to which actors attached a meaning.

• Long Answer (LA) Type Questions

1. What are the main features of the theory of alienation?

Ans. Karl Marx argued that the history of mankind is characterised by increasing control of man over nature which led to the increasing alienation of man. Alienation is a condition in which men are dominated by the forces of their own creation and which confronts them with alien powers.

The main features of alienation are as follows

    (i) In the case of a capitalistic society alienation controls every institutional sphere like economy, polity and even religion.

    (ii) Out of the different kinds of alienation, Karl Marx thinks economic alienation as the most important one as it is related to everyday activities of human beings.

    (iii) Economic alienation alienates the worker from the subject that he produces and from the process of production and from himself and from the community of the fellows. The worker does not at all feel at ease at the working place while he puts his whole life on the production of the product that he produces. This leads to a feeling of apathy and indifference towards the work and the fellow beings.

    (iv) Human beings are alienated from each other as capitalism individualises previously collective forms of social organisation and as relationships get more and more market-mediated.

    (v) The large mass of working people are alienated from the end product of their labour because workers do not own the products they produce and have no connection to the production of a product. Also the workers have no control over their product.

    (vi) Herbert Marcuse's analysis of one dimensional man mainly analysed the position of the worker with respect to the industry.

    (vii) In the theory of alienation, the worker is not only alienated from himself but also from every other person. Every person is alienated from the other person and is likewise alienated from humans.

2. Discuss the main features of the Marxian concept of social change.

Ans. The main features of the Marxian concept of social change are

(i) Marx's theory of social change is much interlinked with his concept of social classes and class conflicts. The process of social change is the primary focus of Marx's thinking.

(ii) Marx believed that the class struggle was the driving force of social change. Marx and Engels wrote in 'The Communist Manifesto' (1848): "The history of all hitherto existing societies is the history of class struggle."

(iii) Marx believed that "the character of social and cultural forms is influenced by the economic base of society. The mode of production and the relationships that exist between those who own and those who do not own the means of production also influence social change.

(iv) History is the story of conflict between the exploiting and the exploited classes. This conflict repeats itself again and again until capitalism is overthrown by the workers and a socialist state is created. Socialism runs before ultimate social form of communism in any society.

(v) The Marxism theory of social change is essentially conflict-oriented. It is appropriately called the 'Conflict Theory of Change'. Marx as a conflict theorist considered society fundamentally dynamic, not static.

(vi) Marx regards conflict as normal, not as abnormal process and he believes that the existing conditions in any society contain the seeds of future social changes.

3. Define social facts. Mention special rules proposed by Durkheim to study social facts.

Ans. **Meaning of Social Facts** According to Emile Durkheim, sociology is the study of social facts. Social facts are things that are external to an individual and constrain their behaviour. They are general in nature.

They are combined representations of social behaviour of a group of people. Social institutions like law, education and religion also constitute social facts alongwith beliefs, feelings and collective practices.

Durkheim proposed special rules for the study of social facts which are as follows

(i) **Social facts be considered as things** The first step in the special rules is to consider social facts as meaningful things. Thus, he tried to distinguish sociological analysis from personal impressions.

(ii) **Discard all pre-notions of pre-conceptions** Secondly, the sociologist must systematically discard all pre-notions and pre-conceptions while studying social facts.

(iii) **A group of phenomena defined in advance by certain common external characteristics** According to Durkheim, each sociological study must have a group of phenomena defined in advance by certain common external characteristics as the subject matter.

(iv) **Investigation independent of individual manifestations** He argued that sociologist must investigate general social facts impacting the whole society, instead of focusing on individual manifestations.

4. Explain in detail the types of authority given by Max Weber.

Ans. Authority is the legal and sanctioned form of power by the state. The term 'sanction' here refers to power which is given approval by the society. Power is generally defined as the capacity of a person to influence the behaviour of the other person against his wish.

There are three types of authority illustrated by Weber. They are as follows

(i) **Legal Authority** It is the authority which is based on formal rules and laws. This type of authority is commanded by the laws and the rules of the country. An authoritative person uses this type of authority according to the definite rules and a person can be punished if he goes beyond his jurisdiction. People who have legal authority don't have the same type of authority and the authority of the concerned person depends upon his post. There also exists a hierarchy among the different posts.

(ii) **Traditional Authority** It is the type of authority which is given on the basis of social values. There are no written laws and rules behind this type of authority. A leader is someone who follows and promotes the existing tradition and established social order. Even though, the leader is a dominant personality the prevalent order in society makes him/her eligible to rule. This kind of leadership could be seen in the authority wielded by the head of the joint family in the Indian family system.

(iii) **Charismatic Authority** This type of authority points to an individual who possesses certain traits that make a leader extraordinary. This type of leader is not only capable of but actually possesses the superior power of charisma to rally diverse and conflict-prone people behind him. Charismatic leadership can be problematic because it is somehow based on some forms of a promise of overhauling of an unjust system. It is not impossible, however, to find such type of a leader in our history. A charismatic leader holds the mission to unite his people in times of difficulty and differences in order to attain an almost impossible goal.

5. Show with examples, how moral codes are indicators of social solidarity? **(NCERT)**

Ans. The following examples show how moral codes are indicators of social solidarity

   (i) **Moral Codes are Imposed by Collective Agreement** According to Durkheim, the social solidarity was to be found in the codes of conduct imposed on individuals by collective agreement. In the everyday life, we can see such practices. For example, in Western societies, people generally wear black dress for funeral. It will be offensive to wear colourful clothes.

   (ii) **Moral Conduct Codes are Manifestations of Particular Social Conditions** It means that morally appropriate condition for one society can be inappropriate for another. For example, pecking (kissing on cheek) is morally appropriate in Western societies, but not in India. According to Durkheim, the prevailing social conditions could be derived from moral codes.

   (iii) **Moral Codes can Predict Behaviour** Construction of choice in social action meant that behaviour can be predict as it follows a pattern. By observing behaviour patterns, it is possible to identify the norms, codes and social solidarities governing them. For example, in India, younger people bow down to touch feet of elder as a mark of respect and humbleness.

6. Can you identify any ideas or theories which have led to the formation of social movements in India in recent times? **(NCERT)**

Ans. Many social ideas/theories have been led to formation of social movements in India after independence. These include theories related to socialism, feminism and environmentalism. These are discussed as follows

   (i) **Socialism** Socialist movements have strived to secure economic justice for backward classes. The ideal of socialism has been recognised in the Preamble of the Constitution of India as well. Dalits and tribals have participated in socio-political movements to acquire political power based on the ideas of social reforms movements of 19th and 20th centuries. These groups had been exploited from ancient time and are now endeavouring to claim their place in society.

   (ii) **Feminism** It seeks to redefine the role of women in society and bring it on equal footing with that of men. Feminist movements have struggled against stereotypes and made efforts to secure the rights of women at home and workplace with some degrees of success.

   (iii) **Environmentalism** Environmental movements have combined environmental and social concerns of people which have been overshadowed by developmental concerns. The Gandhian ideals of peaceful agitation and simplistic living have their association with most of these movements.

- Environmentalism has recently acquired a prominent focus among social concerns with problems like climate change and its attendant costs, particularly for developing countries. Major socio-environmental movements in India are the Chipko movement, the Appiko Movement, Narmada Bachao Andolan and Silent Valley Conservation.

7. Can you think of reasons why we should study the work of thinkers who died long ago? What could be some reasons to not study them? **(NCERT)**

Ans. The work of thinkers who died long ago needs to be studied because it is important to understand the impact of their ideologies in order to know the present-day societies well.

Reasons to study works of early thinkers

   (i) For understanding the communist model and its failures, one needs to study the theories developed by Karl Marx on capitalism and communism.

   (ii) Some theories of scholars are still relevant in the present day societies. The idea of bureaucracy by Max Weber is a very important element of functioning of present day societies.

   (iii) Theories of thinkers also provide many answers to social developments of the past. For example, the progress of Western societies compared to Asian societies can be understood through the study of Protestant-Ethic and the Rise of Capitalism by Max Weber.

   (iv) The difference between sociology and psychology can be understood by the example of study of 'Suicide' done by Emile Durkheim.

Reasons for not studying the works of early thinkers

   (i) Some of the old concepts may not be applicable to the present day societies. This can be attributed to unforeseen changes in social, economic, cultural and technological fields which accompany the advent of a new era. For instance, the theory of Karl Marx where he concludes that the working class would protest against the capitalist and a new form of socialist regime would emerge, was eventually proved wrong and later the theory of Max Weber was accepted.

   (ii) There are many critics to Karl Marx's theory. For example, the ideology of the Indian villages being self-sufficient entity by the Western scholars, was highly criticised by the Indians.

8. What are the basic features of bureaucracy?

(**NCERT**)

Ans. Bureaucratic authority is characterised by following features

Functioning of Officials Within the bureaucracy, officials have fixed areas of '**official jurisdiction**' governed by rules, laws and administrative regulations. The regular activities of the bureaucratic organisation are distributed in a fixed way as official duties. Moreover, commands are issued by higher authorities for implementation by subordinates in a stable way, but the responsibilities of officials are strictly delimited by the authority available to them.

Hierarchical Ordering of Positions Authority and **office** are generally placed on a graded hierarchy where the higher officials supervise the lower ones. This allows scope of appeal to a higher official in case of dissatisfaction with the decisions of lower officials.

Reliance on Written Document Management of a **bureaucratic organisation** is carried out on the basis of written documents which are preserved as records. These documents are also a part of the public domain which is separate from the private life of the officials.

Office Management As it is a specialised and modern activity, it requires trained and skilled personnel to conduct operations.

Conduct in Office Official's conduct in office is governed by exhaustive rules and regulations that are usually pre-decided by the government. These separate his/her public conduct from his/her behaviour in the private domain. Also since, these rules and regulations have legal recognition, officials can be held accountable.

Weber argued that individual requires high-level skills and specialisations, as it forms the basis of modern society. The legal boundation on officials prevented them from exercising unlimited power and made them accountable to their clients. Because the work was carried out in the public domain.

9. Read the following paragraph and answer the question that follow.

Capitalist society was marked by an ever intensifying process of alienation operating at several levels. First, modern capitalist society is one where humans are more alienated from nature than ever before; second, human beings are alienated from each other as capitalism individualises previously collective forms of social organisation and as relationships get more and more market-mediated. Third, the large mass of working people is alienated from the fruits of its labour because workers do not own the products they produce. Moreover, workers have no control over the work process itself — unlike in the days when skilled craftsmen controlled their own labour, today the

content of the factory worker's working day is decided by the management. Finally, as the combined result of all these alienations, human beings are also alienated from themselves and struggle to make their lives meaningful in a system where they are both more free but also more alienated and less in control of their lives than before.

What is a capitalist society? What is a modern capitalist society? How is a human being alienated due to the effects of capitalism?

Ans. A modern capitalist society is characterised by the intensifying process of alienation. Unlike other societies, human beings experience alienation at different levels in capitalism. This factor alone differentiates the modern capitalist society from all others. Human beings are alienated in the following manner under capitalism

- The factory system renders the workers working within the bounds of the factor and this alienated them from nature. Unlike in the case of primitive society where humans worked with nature through agricultural activities.

- Human beings or workers are also alienated from one another. As they are involved in minimal social interaction while working. The relationship they share becomes market-mediated.

- The workers or human beings are alienated from the product they produce and the production process. Even with the hard labour, they put into the production of goods they are incapable of owning these products. At the same time, they have no control over the production process.

- Ultimately, the collective impact of the above-mentioned levels of alienation leads to human beings alienated from themselves or from realising their true potential. They become part of a broad production process where every aspect of their job is pre-decided for them. The mechanical way of labour pushes them further away from their true human nature.

- The above-mentioned points a projects clear idea concerning the nature of modern capitalist society and the kind of impact it has on the social structure of society.

10. Read the following paragraph and answer the question that follow.

Apart from empathetic understanding, Weber also suggested another methodological tool for doing sociology — the 'ideal type'. An ideal type is a logically consistent model of a social phenomenon that highlights its most significant characteristics. Being a conceptual tool designed to help analysis, it is not meant to be an exact reproduction of reality. Ideal types may exaggerate some features of phenomenon that are considered to be analytically important, and ignore or downplay others. Obviously, an ideal type should correspond to reality in a broad sense, but its main job is to assist analysis by bringing out important features and connections of the social phenomenon being studied. An ideal type is to be judged by how helpful it is for analysis and understanding, not by how accurate or detailed a description it provides.

What did Max Weber suggest the sociologists? What do you understand by ideal type mentioned in the passage? What importance ideal types carry for sociologists?

Ans. Max Weber suggested the sociologists a methodological tool for social analysis along with having empathetic understanding. He laid the foundation of interpretive sociology based on empathetic understanding. From the above-mentioned paragraph, it could be understood that the ideal type is a kind of tool used for social analysis. It is a conceptual tool that ought to be used by sociologists to interpret and analyse social phenomena. As per Weber, an ideal type is to be treated as a medium to enhance understanding not to judge how accurately it describes the social reality.

An ideal type carries the following importance to a sociologist

- It could aid analysis, study and enhance understanding of social phenomena.
- It could assist sociologists in bringing out the important features and connections of the social phenomena being studied.
- It helps to develop a broad idea of reality. An ideal type does reproduce reality but it could exaggerate, downplay, or even ignore certain aspects of social phenomena if it helps in the understanding of the same.
- It could be used as a reference to understand a social phenomenon.

• Case-Based Questions

1. Read the following passage and answer the questions.

The presence of ideology is one reason why the relationship between economic and socio-political processes becomes complicated. In every epoch, the ruling classes promote a dominant ideology. This dominant ideology or way of seeing the world, tends to justify the domination of the ruling class and the existing social order.

However, dominant ideologies are not always successful, and they can also be challenged by alternative worldviews or rival ideologies. As consciousness spreads unevenly among classes, how a class will act in a particular historical situation cannot be pre-determined. Hence, according to him, economic processes generally tend to generate class conflicts, though this also depends on political and social conditions. Given favourable conditions, class conflicts culminate in revolutions.

(i) Whose ideas are highlighted in the given passage? What did he consider as the foundation of every social system?

Ans. The ideas of Karl Marx are highlighted in the given passage. Marx believed that economic structures and processes are the foundation of every social system throughout human history.

(ii) Which concept is implied by the word consciousness in the above passage? Identify and define the same.

Ans. Marx defined class consciousness as a state when a class becomes subjectively aware of their identity and interests. And thereby, they become aware of their rival's class identity and interests as well.

(iii) In a capitalist society, which class needs to develop an "alternate ideology"? Did Marx refer to the given class as bourgeoisie?

Ans. In a capitalist society, the working class needs to develop an alternate or rival ideology. No, Marx referred to the dominant/ruling/capitalist class as the bourgeoisie who owns the modes of production in capitalist society.

2. Read the following passage and answer the questions.

At a more specific level, we can think of the mode of production as being something like a building in the sense that it consists of a foundation or base, and a superstructure or something erected on top of the base. The base — or economic base — is primarily economic and includes the productive forces and production relations. Productive forces refer to all the means or factors of production such as land, labour, technology, sources of energy (such as electricity, coal, petroleum and so on). Production relations refer to all the economic relationships and forms of a labour organisation that are involved in production. Production relations are also property relations or relationships based on the ownership or control of the means of production.

(i) As per Karl Marx in a capitalist society, what is constituted as superstructure? Which factor or base determined the superstructure?

Ans. According to Karl Marx, the institutions like religion, art, law, literature or different forms of beliefs and ideas were all part of the superstructure. Marx argued that the economic base determined and informed the superstructure in a capitalist society.

(ii) From the information provided in the given passage, what would the production relations and productive forces in a primitive society be comprised of?

Ans. In a primitive society, the productive forces consisted of nature — forests, lands, animals and so on — along with very rudimentary forms of technology like simple stone tools and hunting weapons. Production relations were based on community property and included tribal forms of hunting or gathering.

(iii) In a capitalist mode of production, the production relations favoured the working class. Is this statement true? If yes/no why?

Ans. This statement is false because the relations of production favoured the ruling class or the bourgeoisie in a capitalist mode of production. The bourgeoisie owned the lands and controlled the means of production. The working class is the victim of capitalist society.

3. Read the following passage and answer questions.

Weber used the ideal type to illustrate the three types of authority that he defined as traditional, charismatic and rational-legal. While the source of traditional authority was custom and precedence, charismatic authority derived from divine sources or the 'gift of grace', and rational-legal authority was based on the legal demarcation of authority. The legal authority which prevailed in modern times was epitomised in 'X'. 'X' was a mode of organisation that was premised on the separation of the public from the domestic world. This meant that behaviour in the public domain was regulated by explicit rules and regulations. Moreover, as a public institution, it also restricted the power of the officials concerning their responsibilities and did not provide absolute power to them. Weber characterised it as a modern form of political authority because it demonstrated how an individual actor was both recognised for her/his skills and training and given responsibilities with the requisite authority to implement them.

(i) What does X in the above passage stands for? Identify and define the same.

Ans. The X in the above passage stands for bureaucracy. As per Weber, bureaucracy is a mode of organisation based on the rational-legal authority and the separation of the public from the domestic world.

(ii) As Bureaucracy is a specialised and modern activity what kind of personnel it required to conduct operations?

Ans. As it is a specialised and modern activity it require trained and skilled personnel to conduct operations.

(iii) What is the nature of authority associated with bureaucracy as per Weber? And why?

Ans. Weber stated that bureaucracy epitomises rational-legal authority. Rational-legal authority is based on the demarcation of authority and bureaucracy restricts and demarks the power of officials based on their responsibilities.

Chapter Test

Multiple Choice Questions

1. —— evolved in the 19th century in Western Europe as a result of —— changes that took place three centuries ago changing the way people lived.
   (a) Enlightenment, rational
   (b) Sociology, revolutionary
   (c) The French Revolution, rational
   (d) The Industrial Revolution, technological

2. The French Revolution announced the arrival of ——— at the level of individuals and ———.
   (a) political sovereignty, nation-state
   (b) social freedom, nation-state
   (c) governance, nation-state
   (d) rationality, nation-state

3. Serfs are associated with which of the following modes of production?
   (a) Capitalist
   (b) Primitive Communism
   (c) Feudal system
   (d) Slavery

4. Max Weber believed that capitalism is a necessary and progressive stage of human history. Which part in this statement is invalid?
   (a) Max Weber believed
   (b) Capitalism is necessary
   (c) progressive stage of human history
   (d) All parts are valid

5. Bureaucracy is a type of mode of production. Which part of this statement is invalid?
   (a) type of
   (b) Bureaucracy
   (c) mode of production
   (d) All parts are valid

Short Answer Type Questions

6. List any four features of bureaucracy.
7. What is the importance of enlightenment for the development of sociology?
8. Explain the meaning of collective consciousness.
9. Explain what do you understand by historical materialism.
10. What is the meaning of traditional action defined by Max Weber?

Long Answer Type Questions

11. Discuss briefly the contributions of Emile Durkheim to the field of sociology.
12. Discuss Weber's concept of class, status and party.
13. What are the various causes of division of labour?
14. Explain the various factors that have contributed to the development of bureaucracy.

Answers

1. (b)   *2.* (a)   *3.* (c)   *4.* (a)   *5.* (c)

Indian Sociologists

In this Chapter...

Development of Sociology in India

In India, the development of sociology began in 1919 at the **University of Bombay**. After that in 1920, two other universities i.e. **Calcutta** and **Lucknow** also began programmes of teaching and research in sociology and anthropology.

In the early days, there was no idea of how Indian sociology would be shaped. With time, sociology became a challenging discipline in the Indian context. Western sociology slowly started emerging and tried to make sense of modernity in the Indian context. India first witnessed modernity in the colonial era when it was ruled by the British Government.

Some sociologists who played key role in Indian sociology are LK Ananthakrishna Iyer, Sarat Chandra Roy, Govind Sadashiv Ghurye, DP Mukerji, AR Desai and MN Srinivas. These sociologists are discussed as follows

LK Ananthakrishna Iyer (1861-1937)

LK Ananthakrishna Iyer was one of the pioneers of social anthropology in India. He began his career as a clerk, later became a college teacher in Cochin State (present day in Kerala).

Ananthakrishna Iyer did the work for British government in an ethnographic survey. During this survey, he was working as a college teacher in the Maharajah's college at Ernakulam, and also functioning as the unpaid Superintendent of Ethnography during the weekends. His works was highly appreciated by British anthropologists and administrators of that period and later he was also invited to help with a similar ethnographic survey in Mysore State.

Although, he did not posses to a sociological background, he made attempts in popularising sociology as a discipline in India. He was probably the first self-taught anthropologist to receive national and international recognition as a scholar and an academician.

At University of Calcutta, he was appointed as a Reader and worked between 1917-1932. There, he helped to set up the **first post-graduate anthropology department in India**. He had no formal qualifications in anthropology, but he was elected as the President of the Ethnology section of the Indian Science Congress.

He was awarded with an honorary doctorate by German University during his lecture tour of European Universities. He was also conferred the titles of **Rao Bahadur** and **Dewan Bahadur** by Cochin State.

Sarat Chandra Roy (1871-1942)

Sarat Chandra Roy was a lawyer as well as anthropologist who pioneered the discipline of sociology in India. Before taking his law degree from Calcutta's Ripon College, Roy had done graduate and post-graduate degrees in English.

He went to Ranchi in 1898 and took a job of English teacher at a Christian Missionary School. In Ranchi, he became the leading authority on the culture and society of the tribal people of the Chhotanagpur region (present day Jharkhand).

Roy's interest in anthropological matters began when he gave up his school job and began practising law at the Ranchi courts. Later, he was appointed as official interpreter in the court.

He became deeply interested in tribal society. He travelled extensively among tribal communities, did intensive fieldwork among them and wrote many valuable monographs[1] and research articles.

He published more than one hundred articles in leading Indian and British academic journals in addition to his famous monographs on the **Oraon**, the **Mundas** and the **Kharias**. He founded the journal **Man in India** in 1922, which is still published.

Govind Sadashiv (GS) Ghurye (1893-1983)

He is regarded as founder of **institutionalised sociology**[2] in India. He was also the head of India's first post-graduate teaching department of Sociology at Bombay University for 35 years. He was also the founder of the **Indian Sociological Society**. Its journal **Sociological Bulletin**[3] was launched in 1952.

Ghurye's Bombay University department was the first to successfully implement the features that laid foundation of sociology as a discipline. These were as follows

(*i*) The active combining of teaching and research within the same institution.

(*ii*) The merger of social anthropology and sociology into a composite discipline.

He wrote on a broad range of themes including tribes; kinship, family, caste, marriage, culture, civilisation and the historic role of cities, religion, sociology of conflict and integration and race.

Ghurye and Tribals of India

Ghurye's writings on tribes and his debate with **Verrier Elwin** made him known to the academic world. In the 1930s and 1940s, there was much debate on the place of tribal societies within India and how the state should respond to them.

Many British **administrator-anthropologists**[4] were specially interested in the tribes of India and believed them to be primitive people with a distinctive culture different from mainstream Hinduism. They also believed that the innocent and simple tribals would suffer exploitation and cultural degradation through contact with Hindu culture and society.

The British felt that the state had a duty to protect the tribes and maintain their way of life and culture who were facing constant pressure to assimilate with mainstream Hindu culture. However, nationalist Indians were equally passionate about their belief in the unity of India and the need for modernising Indian society and culture. They believed that attempts to preserve tribal culture were misguided and resulted in maintaining tribals in a backward state as 'museums' of primitive culture.

As many features of Hinduism itself felt to be backward and in need of reform, they felt that tribes, too, needed to develop.

Ghurye became the best-known interpreter of the nationalist view and insisted that the tribes of India should be regarded as **backward Hindus** rather than culturally distinct groups.

He interacted with many tribal cultures to show that they had been involved in constant interactions with Hinduism over a long period. Thus, they lag behind in the same process of **assimilation**[5] , that all Indian communities had gone through.

The **protectionists** (protectors of tribals) believed that assimilation of tribals in society would result in their severe exploitation and cultural extinction. On the other hand, Ghurye and the nationalists argued that these ill-effects were not specific to tribal cultures, but were common to all the backward and downtrodden sections of Indian society.

G.S. Ghurye on Race and Caste

Ghurye in his book *Caste and Race in India* (1932), provided a detailed critique of the dominant theories about the relationship between race and caste.

Herbert Risley, (a British colonial official) became the main supporter of the view of Ghurye on race and caste theories.

---

1 **Monograph** A monograph is a highly detailed and documented (or written) study on a specific topic, field, or subject.

2 **Institutionalised sociology** This term implies making sociology into a formal discipline that is being taught at the college or university level.

3 **Sociological Bulletin** Sociological Bulletin is an official journal of Indian Sociological societies founded by G.S. Ghurye. It comprises articles, studies, research papers, etc., on the wide-ranging subject matter of sociology.

4 **Administrator-anthropologists** The term refers to British administrative officials who were part of the British Indian government in the 19th and early 20th centuries, and who took great interest in conducting anthropological research, specially surveys and censuses.

5 **Assimilation** A process by which one culture gradually absorbs another.

According to this view, human beings can be divided into distinct and separate races on the basis of their physical characteristics such as the circumference of the skull, the length of the nose, or the volume (size) of the cranium or the part of the skull where the brain is located.

Risley believed that India was a unique laboratory (place of experiment) for studying the evolution of racial types because caste-based Indian society strictly prohibits inter-marriage among different groups. Risley's main argument was that caste must have originated in race because different caste groups seemed to belong to distinct racial types.

In general, the higher castes belong to Indo-Aryan racial traits, while the lower castes seems to belong to non-Aryan aboriginal, Mongoloid or other racial groups.

On the basis of extensive research, i.e. difference between groups in terms of average measurements for length of nose, size of cranium, etc., they concluded that lower castes were the aboriginal inhabitants of India and had been **subjugated**[6] by Aryan people who were settled in India from somewhere else.

Ghurye agreed with the basic argument put forward by Risley but also believed it to be only partially correct. Ghurye believed that Risley's thesis of the upper castes being Aryan and the lower castes being non-Aryan was broadly true only for Northern India.

In other parts of India, the inter-group differences in the **anthropometric measurements**[7] were not very large or systematic. This suggested that, in most of India except the Indo-Gangetic plain, different racial groups had been mixing with each other for a very long time. Thus, the 'racial purity' had been preserved only in North India due to the prohibition on **inter-marriage**[8].

In the rest of the country, the practice of **endogamy** (marrying only within a particular caste group) may have been introduced into groups that were already racially varied. Today, the racial theory of caste is no longer believed, but in the first half of the 20th century, it was still considered to be true.

Features of Caste Defined by Ghurye

Ghurye is also known for offering a comprehensive definition of caste. His definition emphasises six features.

These are as follows

(*i*) **Caste is an institution based on segmental division** It means that caste society is divided into a number of closed, mutually exclusive segments or compartments. Each caste is one such compartment. It is closed because caste is decided by birth — the children born to parents of a particular caste will always belong to that caste. A person's caste can neither be avoided nor changed.

(*ii*) **Caste society is based on hierarchical division** Each caste is strictly unequal to every other caste, i.e. every caste is either higher or lower than every other one. In theory (though not in practice), no two castes are ever equal.

(*iii*) **Caste system involves restrictions on social interaction** The institution of caste necessarily involves restrictions on social interaction, specially the sharing of food. There are different rules prescribing what kind of food may be shared between which groups. These rules are governed by ideas of purity and pollution. Some rules also apply to social interaction. For example, in untouchability, the touch of people of particular castes is thought to be polluting.

(*iv*) **Caste involves rights and duties** Caste also involves differential rights and duties for different castes. These rights and duties apply not only to religious practices but extend to the secular world. As per the ethnographic accounts, interaction between people of different castes are governed by these rules.

(*v*) **Caste restricts the choice of occupation** Caste is decided by birth and is hereditary. At the level of society, caste functions as a form of the division of labour in which specific occupations are being allocated to specific castes.

(*vi*) **Caste involves strict restrictions on marriage** People of a caste marry only within the caste. They follow rules about **exogamy**[9] or whom one may not marry. This combination of rules about eligible and non-eligible groups helps reproduce the caste system.

Ghurye's above definitions helped to make the study of caste more systematic. His conceptual definition was based on what the classical texts prescribed. In actual practice, many of these features of caste were changing, though all of them continue to exist in some forms.

---

6   **Subjugated** Subjugation is a kind of oppression experienced by a group of people by another dominant group.

7   **Anthropometric measurements** are noninvasive quantitative measurements of the body. The core elements of anthropometry are height, weight, head circumference, body mass index, body circumferences to assess for adiposity and skinfold thickness.

8   **Inter-marriage** Marriage between people of different religions, castes, tribes, social groups, etc.

9   **Exogamy** A social institution that defines the boundary of a social group with which or within which marriage relations are prohibited; marriages must be contracted outside these prohibited groups.

Govind Sadashiv Ghurye (1893-1983)

GS Ghurye was born on 12th December, 1893 in Malvan town of the Konkan coastal region of Western India. His family owned a trading business which later declined.

Timeline of the Events in the Life of Ghurye

1913 : He joined Elphinstone College in Bombay and received Sanskrit Honours for the B.A. degree and M.A. degree in Sanskrit and English 1916 and 1918, respectively.

1919 : He was selected for a scholarship by the University of Bombay for training abroad in sociology. Initially, he went to the London School of Economics to study with LT Hobhouse. Later went to Cambridge to study with WHR Rivers, and was deeply influenced by his diffusionist perspective.

1923 : His Ph.D. was submitted under AC Haddon after River's sudden death in 1922. He returned to Bombay in May.

Caste and Race in India, the manuscript based on the doctoral **dissertation**[10], was accepted for publication in a major book series at Cambridge.

1924 : He was appointed Reader and Head of the Department of Sociology at Bombay University in June.

1983 : G S Ghurye died at the age of 90.

Sociology between the 1920s and the 1950s

Sociology in India was equated with the two major departments at Bombay and Lucknow between the 1920s and the 1950s. Both were began as combined departments of sociology and economics. While the Bombay department in this period was led by GS Ghurye, the Lucknow department had three major figures, the famous 'trinity' of **Radhakamal Mukerjee** (the founder), **DP Mukerji** and **DN Majumdar**. Among these personalities DP Mukerji was the most popular. His perspective and contribution to Indian sociology is discussed below.

Dhurjati Prasad (DP) Mukerji (1894-4961)

DP Mukerji was among the most influential scholars of his generation not only in sociology but in intellectual and public life beyond the academics. His influence and popularity came not so much from his scholarly writings as from his teaching, his speaking at academic events, and his work in the media, including newspaper articles and radio programmes.

He had an active interest in a variety of subjects like literature, music, film, Western and Indian philosophy, Marxism, political economy and development planning. DP Mukerji wrote many books in English and Bengali. His pioneering work which is considered a classic in its genre was **Introduction to Indian Music**. Dhurjati Prasad Mukerji was strongly influenced by Marxism but he viewed it as a tool for social analysis rather than a political programme for action.

DP Mukerji on Tradition and Change

DP Mukerji believed that the distinctive feature of India was its social system. So, it is the primary duty of an Indian sociologist to study and to know the social traditions of India.

For DP Mukerji, this study of tradition was not oriented only towards the past, but also included sensitivity to change. Thus, tradition was a living tradition. It maintains its links with the past, also adapt to the present and thus, changing over time.

DP Mukerji believed that sociologists should learn and be familiar with both 'high' and 'low' languages and cultures.

He believed that Indian society and culture were not individualistic in the Western sense, because the Indian social system was based on collective sect, or caste-action, instead of individual (**voluntaristic**[11]) action. According to D.P. Mukerji, the basic meaning of the word tradition implies to transmit.

Traditions are strongly rooted in the past that is kept alive through stories and myth. This link with the past does prevent change, as internal and external sources of changes are always present in society. Society learns to adapt to these changes. As per D.P., the economy is a major internal source of change in Western societies, but this source is ineffective in India.

DP Mukerji believed that class conflict has been 'smoothed and covered by caste traditions' in the Indian context. According to him, one of the first tasks of Indian sociology is to provide an account of internal and non-economic causes of social change.

---

10 Dissertation It is a long piece of academic writing based on original veseralh.

11 Voluntaristic Voluntaristic represents a viewpoint that individuals are free to act and achieve their goals with the existing social and cultural restrictions/constraints.

Dhurjati Prasad Mukerji (1894-1961)

DP Mukerji was born on 5th October, 1894 in a middle class Bengali Brahmin family. He received undergraduate degree in science and post-graduate degrees in History and Economics from Calcutta University.

Timeline of the Events in the Life of Dhurjati Prasad Mukerji

1924 : He was appointed as Lecturer in the Department of Economics and Sociology at Lucknow University.

1938 : He became Director of Information under the first Congress-led government of the United Provinces of British India (present day Uttar Pradesh).

1947 : He served as a Member of the U.P. Labour Enquiry Committee.

1949 : He was appointed as a Professor (by special order of the Vice Chancellor) at Lucknow University.

1953 : He was appointed as a Professor of Economics at Aligarh Muslim University.

1955 : He gave Presidential Address to the newly formed Indian Sociological Society.

1956 : He underwent major surgery for throat cancer in Switzerland.

1961 : He died on 5th December, 1961.

Principles of Social Change

According to DP Mukerji, there were three principles of change recognised in Indian tradition namely *Anubhava, Shruti* and *Smriti*.

Anubhava or personal experience is the revolutionary and important principle. However, in the Indian context personal experience soon changed into collective experience of groups. This generalised *Anubhava* or the collective experience of groups become important.

The high traditions are centred in *Smriti* (memory) and *Shruti* (what is heared). They are periodically challenged by collective experience of groups and sects. e.g., in Bhakti Movement.

He emphasised that this was true about both Hindu and Muslim culture in India. In Indian context, discursive reason (*buddhi-vichar*) is the dominant force for change, but *Anubhava* and *Prem* (experience and love) have been historically superior as agents of change.

In a caste-based society, the process of change or **rebellion**[12] is contained within the limits of overarching tradition, and it prevents the formation of classes and class consciousness. Mukerji's viewpoint of change and tradition made him to criticise the blindly borrowing of concepts from the Western intellectual tradition. He believed like tradition; modernity was needed but not blindly adopted. D.P Mukerji was a proud but critical inherit of tradition and an admiring critic of modernity.

Akshay Ramanlal (AR) Desai (1915-1994)

AR Desai was a Marxist who joined the Bombay Sociology department to study under the guidance of Ghurye . He was directly involved in politics, but later resigned from his membership of the Communist Party of India. He wrote his doctoral dissertation on the *Social Aspects of Indian Nationalism*. In 1948, his **thesis** was published as the *Social Background of Indian Nationalism*.

In this book, he offered a Marxist analysis of Indian nationalism, which gave prominence to economic processes and divisions, while taking account of the specific conditions of **British colonialism**[13]. Although, it had its critics, this book proved to be very popular and went through numerous reprints. Among the other themes that Desai worked on were peasant movements, rural sociology, modernisation, urban issues, political sociology, forms of the state and human rights. AR Desai was elected President of the Indian Sociological Society.

AR Desai on the State

In his essay, *The Myth of the Welfare State*, Desai provides a detailed **critique**[14] of capitalist state by pointing out its numerous shortcomings.

Desai identified the unique features of the welfare state. These are as follows

(*i*) **It is a Positive State** It means that, unlike the 'laissez faire'[15] of classical liberal political theory, the welfare state does not seek to do only the minimum necessary things to maintain law and order. The welfare state is an interventionist state and actively uses its considerable powers to design and implement social policies for the betterment of society.

(*ii*) **It is a Democratic State** Democracy was considered an essential condition for the emergence of the welfare state. Formal democratic institutions such as multi-party elections are defining features of the welfare state. The liberal thinkers excluded socialist and communist states form this definition.

---

12 Rebellion is the act of rejecting social and cultural goals and wanting to replace them with new ones. In other words, attempting to replace the existing social and cultural norms.

13 British colonialism British colonialism represents how the British used to indirectly govern their colonies. India was one of the colonies of British.

14 Critique A critique represents the good and bad side concerning a topic, idea, social reality, or anything.

15 Laissez Faire A French phrase (literally 'let be' or 'leave alone') that stands for a political and economic doctrine that advocates minimum state intervention in the economy and economic relations; usually associated with belief in the regulative powers and efficiency of the free market.

(iii) **It involves a Mixed Economy** A mixed economy means an economy where both private capitalist enterprises and state or publicly owned enterprises co-exist. A welfare state does not eliminate the capitalist market or prevent public investment in industry and other fields. In welfare state, state sector concentrates on basic goods and social infrastructure, while private industry dominates the consumer goods sector.

Criteria for Measuring Performance of Welfare State

AR Desai suggested some test criteria by which the performance of the welfare state can be measured.

These are as follows

(i) Welfare state should ensure freedom from poverty, social discrimination and security for all its citizen.

(ii) Welfare state should remove inequalities of income through measures to redistribute income from the rich to the poor, and by preventing the concentration of wealth.

(iii) Welfare state should transform the economy in such a way that the capitalist profit motive is made subservient (or less important) to the real needs of the community.

(iv) Welfare state should ensure stable development free from the cycle of economic booms and depressions.

(v) Welfare state should provide employment for all.

Using these criteria, Desai examines the performance of those states that are most often described as welfare states, such as Britain, the USA and much of Europe.

Most modern capitalist states, even in the most developed countries, fail to provide minimum levels of economic and social security to all their citizens. They are unable to reduce economic inequality and often seem to encourage it.

The welfare states have also been unsuccessful at enabling stable development free from market fluctuations. The presence of excess economic capacity and high levels of unemployment is yet another failure. Based on these arguments, Desai concludes that the notion of the welfare state is a myth.

AR Desai cites many Marxist thinkers to emphasise the importance of democracy even under communism. He argued strongly that political liberties and the rule of law must be upheld in all genuinely socialist states.

Akshay Ramanlal Desai (1915-1994)

A R Desai was born in 1915. He got early education in Baroda, then in Surat and Bombay.

Timeline of the Events in the Life of Akshay Ramanlal Desai

1934-39: He served as a member of Communist Party of India and was involved with Trotskyite groups.

1946 : His Ph.D. was submitted at Bombay under the supervision of GS Ghurye.

1951 : He joined as a faculty of the Department of Sociology at Bombay University

1953-1981: He served as a member of Revolutionary Socialist Party.

1961 : His book 'Rural Transition in India' was published.

1967 : He was appointed as a Professor and Head of Department.

1975 : 'State and Society in India: Essays in Dissent' was published.

1976 : He retired from Department of Sociology.

1979 : 'Peasant Struggles in India' was published.

1986 : 'Agrarian Struggles in India after Independence' was published.

1994 : He died on 12th November, 1994.

Mysore Narasimhachar (MN) Srinivas

MN Srinivas is the best-known Indian sociologist of post-independence era. He owns two doctoral degrees, one from Bombay University and other from Oxford. He was a student of Ghurye's at Bombay. Srinivas' intellectual orientation was transformed by the years he spent at the Department of Social Anthropology in Oxford.

British social anthropology was at that time the dominant force in Western anthropology and Srinivas enjoyed this study by being at the 'centre' of the discipline.

Srinivas' doctoral dissertation was published as *Religion and Society among the Coorgs of South India*. This book established Srinivas' international reputation with its detailed ethnographic application of the **Structural Functional Perspective. It is a perspective in sociology that suggests society is composed of various parts and each part performs relevant functions to maintain social order and stability, dominant in British social anthropology.**

Srinivas was appointed to a newly created lectureship in Indian sociology at Oxford, but resigned in 1951 to return to India as the head of a newly created department of sociology at the Maharaja Sayajirao University at Baroda.

In 1959, he moved to Delhi to set up another department at the Delhi School of Economics, which soon became known as one of the leading centres of sociology in India.

MN Srinivas on the Village

Srinivas had a life-long interest in the Indian village and village society. Although, he visited many villages for a short period, but his interest in villages was developed after his fieldwork for a year at a village near Mysore where he acquired first hand experience of village society. This fieldwork experience proved to be crucial for his career and his intellectual path.

Srinivas was keen in making village studies the dominant field in Indian sociology. Srinivas encouraged a major collective effort at producing detailed ethnographic accounts of village society during the 1950s and 1960s. Alongwith other scholars like **SC Dube** and **DN Majumdar**, Srinivas contributed in making village studies the dominant field in Indian sociology.

Srinivas' writings on the village were of two types

- (*i*) Ethnographic accounts of fieldwork done in villages or discussions of such accounts.
- (*ii*) Historical and conceptual discussions about the Indian village as a unit of social analysis. In these writings, Srinivas was involved in a debate about the usefulness of the village as a concept.

Views of Srinivas and Louis Dumont on Villages

Arguing against the relevance of village studies in social anthropology, Louis Dumont, a social anthropologist, claimed that social institutions like caste were more important than a village. As the village represents a mere collection of people living in a particular area.

People may move from one village to another, but their social institutions, like caste or religion, follows them and goes with them wherever they go. For this reason, Dumont believed that it would be misleading to give much importance to the village as a subject matter of sociology.

Srinivas was against the belief of Dumont and believed that the village was a relevant social entity.

Srinivas also criticised the British administrator-anthropologists who had put forward a picture of the Indian village as unchanging, self-sufficient and little republics. Using historical and sociological evidence, Srinivas showed that the village had experienced considerable change. Moreover, villages were never self-sufficient, and had been involved in various kinds of economic, social and political relationships at the regional level.

Village as a Site of Research

The village as a site of research offered many advantages to Indian sociology. These are as follows

- It provided an opportunity to illustrate the importance of ethnographic research methods.
- It offered eye-witness accounts of the rapid social change that was taking place in the Indian countryside as the newly independent nation began a programme of planned development.
- Village studies provided a new role for a discipline like sociology in the context of an independent nation.
- Rather than being restricted to the study of **primitive people**[16], it could also be made relevant to a modernising society.

Mysore Narasimhachar Srinivas (1916-1999)

Mysore Narasimhachar Srinivas was born on 16th November, 1916 in an Iyengar Brahmin family in Mysore. His father was a landowner and worked for the Mysore power and light department. His early education was at Mysore University and he later went to Bombay to do an MA under GS Ghurye.

Timeline of the Events in the Life of Srinivas

1942 :	His M.A. thesis on Marriage and Family Among the Coorgs was published as book.
1944 :	His Ph.D. thesis (in 2 volumes) was submitted to Bombay University under the supervision of GS Ghurye.
1945 :	He went Oxford and studied first under Radcliffe-Brown and then under Evans-Pritchard.
1947 :	He was awarded D.Phil. degree in Social Anthropology from Oxford and returned to India.
1948 :	He was appointed as a Lecturer in Indian Sociology at Oxford. He spend the year in doing fieldwork in Rampura.
1959 :	He took up Professorship at the Delhi School of Economics to set up the sociology department there.
1971 :	He went Delhi University to co-found the Institute of Social and Economic Change at Bangalore.
1999 :	He died on 30th November, 1999.

Conclusion

The discipline of sociology got a distinctive character by many Indian sociologist, especially by the four sociologists namely, Govind Sadashiv Ghurye, DP Mukerjee, AR Desai and MN Srinivas. By the efforts of these sociologists, sociology was **Indianised**[17].

---

16 Primitive People Primitive people are people belonging to primitive society.

17 Indianised Indianised means to indianise something by giving it in Indian context or by adding Indian character, features, etc.

Chapter Practice

Objective Questions

• Multiple Choice Questions

1. From which of the following universities the development of Sociology started in India?
(a) Madras University (b) Lucknow University
(c) University of Bombay (d) Delhi University

Ans. (c) The development of Sociology started in India from the University of Bombay.

2. The term 'Accidental Anthropologist' is associated with________.
(a) L.K. Ananthakrishna Iyer
(b) Sarat Chandra Roy
(c) Both of the above
(d) None of the above

Ans. (c) The term 'Accidental Anthropologist' is associated with L.K. Ananthakrishna Iyer and Sarat Chandra Roy.

3. The branch of anthropology that studies human racial types is known as______.
(a) Anthropocentric (b) Socio-anthropology
(c) Anthropometry (d) Both (b) and (c)

Ans. (c) Anthropometry is the branch of anthropology that studies human racial types by measuring the human body, such as the volume of the skull, the circumference of the head and the length of nose.

4. Who founded the journal 'Man in India'?
(a) Sarat Chandra Roy (b) GS Ghurye
(c) DP Mukerji (d) None of these

Ans. (a) Sarat Chandra Roy founded the journal 'Man in India' in the year 1922.

5. The institution of caste is based on ____________ as per Ghurye.
(a) Segmental division (b) Hierarchical division
(c) Both (a) and (b) (d) None of these

Ans. (c) As per Ghurye the institution of caste is based on segmental division and hierarchial division. Thus, both (a) and (b) are correct.

6. Risley argued that the higher castes approximated Indo-Aryan racial traits, while the lower castes seemed to belong to non-Aryan aboriginal, Mongoloid or other racial groups. Did Ghurye agree with this?
(a) Ghurye completely agreed with Risley
(b) Ghurye partially agreed with Risley
(c) Ghurye completely disagreed with Risley
(d) None of the above

Ans. (b) Ghurye partially agreed with Risley because his thesis of the upper castes being Aryan and the lower castes being non-Aryan was broadly true only for Northern India.

7. Which of the following statements is not true about the GS Ghurye?
(a) 'Caste and Race in India' is a work of GS Ghurye.
(b) In 1951, GS Ghurye established the Indian Sociological Society.
(c) Ghurye's definition of caste emphasises on features.
(d) According to Ghurye, caste is based on hierarchical division.

Ans (c) Ghurye's definition of caste emphasises on six features. Hence, option (c) is not correct.

8. Which of the following statements is not true about traditions?
(a) Traditions are strongly rooted in past.
(b) Traditions evolve over time by adapting to the present.
(c) D.P. promoted the understanding and study of Indian social traditions.
(d) The root meaning of the word tradition is to diffuse.

Ans (d) Thus, option (d) is not true about traditions.

9. "It is not enough for the Indian sociologist to be a sociologist. He must be an Indian first." This is the quote of ______.
(a) A.R. Desai (b) D.P. Mukerji
(c) M.N. Srinivas (d) G.S. Ghurye

Ans. (b) The above mentioned quote is of D.P. Mukerji. He claimed that Indian sociologists need to be an Indian first, by understanding and sharing the mores, tradition, etc., of Indian society, to become a sociologist.

10. Given the centrality of society in India, it became the first duty of an Indian sociologist to study and to know the social traditions of India. Who said this?

(a) A.P. Desai   (b) R.K. Mukherjee

(c) D.P. Mukerji   (d) G.S. Ghurye

Ans (c) D.P. Mukerji offered centrality to the social traditions of India because he believed that it became the first duty of an Indian sociologist to know social tradition of India. India was its most crucial feature.

11. Marxism influenced the thinking of _____.

(a) D.P. Mukerji   (b) A.R. Desai

(c) Both (a) and (b)   (d) M.N. Srinivas

Ans (c) Marxism influenced the thinking of D.P. Mukerji and A.R. Desai and this influence was reflected in their respective works.

12. ______ concluded that the notion of the ______ is a somewhat of a myth.

(a) R.K. Mukherjee, state   (b) D.P. Mukerji, welfare state

(c) A.R. Desai, welfare state (d) M.N. Srinivas, village

Ans (c) A.R. Desai concluded that the notion of a welfare state is a myth. Most of the states described as welfare states, as per him, are greatly exaggerating this notion.

13. Democracy was considered an essential condition for the emergence of the welfare state. A welfare state involves a mixed economy. What does mixed economy mean here?

(a) An economy where both private enterprises and public enterprises co-exist.

(b) An economy where both private and capitalist enterprises co-exist.

(c) An economy where both public and state-owned enterprises co-exist.

(d) An economy dominated by private enterprises with a minor presence of public enterprises.

Ans (a) A mixed economy represents an economy where both private capitalist enterprises and state or publicly owned enterprises co-exist.

14. In 1959, he moved to Delhi to set up another department at the Delhi School of Economics, which soon became known as one of the leading centres of Sociology in India. Who is he in this context?

(a) G.S. Ghurye   (b) A.R. Desai

(c) M.N. Srinivas   (d) Radha Kamal Mukherjee

Ans (c) He is M.N. Srinivas in the above statement.

15. British administrator-anthropologists painted a picture of Indian village as ________ and _______.

(a) ever-changing, and self-reliant

(b) unchanging, self-sufficient

(c) ever-changing, self-sufficient

(d) unchanging, self-reliant

Ans (b) British administrator-anthropologists painted a picture of Indian village as less importance to a village on an account of it being unchanging and self-sufficient.

• Assertion-Reasoning MCQs

Directions (Q. Nos. 1-3) *Each of these questions contains two statements, Assertion (A) and Reason (R). Each of these questions also has four alternative choices, any one of which is the correct answer. You have to select one of the codes (a), (b), (c) and (d) given below.*

Codes

(a) Both A and R are true and R is the correct explanation of A

(b) Both A and R are true, but R is not the correct explanation of A

(c) A is true, but R is false

(d) A is false, but R is true

1. Assertion (A) Caste is based on hierarchical division.

Reason (R) Each caste is strictly unequal to every other caste, that is, every caste is either higher or lower than every other one.

Ans (a) Ghurye stated that caste is based in a hierarchical division because each caste is strictly unequal i.e. either lower or higher than the other one resulting in ranking amongst them. Hence, both statements are true and R explains A correctly.

2. Assertion (A) D.P. Mukerji believed that there were three principles of change recognised in Indian traditions, namely- Shruti, Smriti, and Anubhava.

Reason (R) In the Indian context, the most important principle of change is personal experience or Anubhava as per D.P. Mukerji

Ans (c) D.P. identified three principles of change in Indian tradition as Shruti, Smriti, and Anubhava. Out of these three, he believed Anubhava or personal experience as the revolutionary principle. But in the Indian context, it was generalised or collective Anubhava, not personalised Anubhava that D.P. considered the most important principle of change. Therefore, A is true and R is false.

3. Assertion (A) The welfare state is a democratic state, as per A.R. Desai.

Reason (R) The welfare state is an interventionist state and actively uses its powers to design and implement social policies for the betterment of society.

Ans (b) A.R. Desai argued that a welfare state is a democratic state where multiparty elections are defining features of the same. Also, a welfare state is an interventionist as it uses power to implement social policies resulting in the betterment of society. Thus, both the statements are true and R is not the correct explanation of A.

• Case Based MCQs

1. Read the following passage carefully and answer the questions.

The root meaning of tradition is to transmit. Its Sanskrit equivalents are either parampara, that is, succession, or aitihya, which comes from the same root as itihas or history. Traditions are thus strongly rooted in the past that are kept alive through the repeated recalling and retelling of stories and myths. However, this link with the past does not rule out change but indicates a process of adaptation to it.

The most commonly cited internal source of change in Western societies is the economy, but this source has not been as effective in India. Class conflict, D.P. believed, had been "smoothed and covered by caste traditions" in the Indian context, where new class relations had not yet emerged very sharply. Based on this understanding, he concluded that one of the first tasks for a dynamic Indian sociology would be to provide an account of the internal, non-economic causes of change.

(i) Who is 'he' in the above-mentioned passage?
(a) A.R. Desai (b) M.N. Srinivas
(c) S.C. Dube (d) D.P. Mukerji

Ans (d) 'He' in the above-mentioned passage refers to D.P. Mukerji.

(ii) The class conflict is not prevalent in the Indian context because________ overpowers the same.
(a) Caste traditions (b) Religious traditions
(c) Both (a) and (b) (d) None of these

Ans (a) The class conflict is not prevalent in the Indian context because of caste traditions overpowers the same.

(iii) As per the above passage, D.P. believed to realise the internal cause of changes we must focus on non-economic causes of change in Indian Sociology because economic factor is not effective in Indian context.
(a) Economic, non-economic factor
(b) Non-economic, change, economic factor
(c) Economic, change, class conflict
(d) Non-economic, change, class conflict

Ans (b) As per the above passage, D.P. believed to realise the internal cause of changes in the Indian context, we must focus on the non-economic causes of change, as economic factors of change are not effective in India, unlike in the West.

2. Read the following passage carefully and answer the questions.

It offered eyewitness accounts of the rapid social change that was taking place in the Indian countryside as the newly independent nation began a programme of planned development. These vivid descriptions of village India were greatly appreciated at the time as urban Indians, as well as policy makers, were able to form impressions of what was going on in the heartland of India. Village studies thus provided a new role for a discipline like Sociology in the context of an independent nation.

(i) The perspective of _______ is mentioned in the above passage, and he was a student of ________.
(a) A.R. Desai, D.P. Mukerji
(b) M.N. Srinivas, G.S. Ghurye
(c) A.R. Desai, G.S. Ghurye
(d) M.N. Srinivas, D.P. Mukerji

Ans (b) The perspective of M.N. Srinivas is mentioned in the above passage, and he was a student of G.S. Ghurye.

(ii) On what claims did M.N. Srinivas prove the relevance of the village as a concept?
(a) He claimed, unlike popular belief, the village is not unchangeable and it has experienced change
(b) He claimed although the village is self-sufficient it is not unchangeable.
(c) Both (a) and (b)
(d) He claimed villages are not unchangeable and self-sufficient. Because it has witnessed change and it had been involved in various economic, social, and political activities at a regional level.

Ans (d) M.N. Srinivas proved the relevance of the village as a concept by refuting the projected notion of it being unchangeable and self-sufficient. Using historical evidence, he showed the changes witnessed in villages and various economic, political, and social activities taking place in villages at a regional level.

(iii) The descriptions of villages were greatly appreciated by the urban Indians and the policy-makers because _____.
(a) it was documented by M.N. Srinivas.
(b) of the popularity of M.N. Srinivas.
(c) it gave an idea about what was going on in villages.
(d) it gave an idea about what M.N. Srinivas was interested in.

Ans. (c) The description of villages was greatly appreciated by the urban Indians and the policy-makers because it gave an impression about what was going on in villages.

Subjective Questions

• Short Answer (SA) Type Questions

1. Who was Sarat Chandra Roy? What was the contribution of Sarat Chandra Roy for tribal society?

Ans. Sarat Chandra Roy was a lawyer and an anthropologist who pioneered the discipline of Sociology in India.

He was deeply interested in tribal society on a bio product of his professional need to interpret tribal customs and laws to the court. Roy travelled extensively among the tribal communities and did intensive work among them and wrote many valuable monography and research articles.

He published more than one hundred articles in leading Indian and British academic journals in addition to his famous monographs on the Oraon, the Mundas, and the Kharias. He also founded the journal 'Man in India' in 1922, which is being published to the present day.

2. What are Govind Sadashiv Ghurye's views about caste and kinship?

Ans. Ghurye in his book *Caste and Race in India* (1932), provided a detailed critique of the dominant theories about the relationship between race and caste. He was concerned with the historical origin of caste and its geographical spread. He also tried to examine the contemporary features including changes in it because of the impact of the British rule. He also explained how India underwent changes in free India.

He recorded the persisting, emerging and the changing features of the complicated caste system in India. He also noted the painful growth of caste patriotism or caste consciousness and the transformation of a caste into community or ethnic group.

Ghurye also developed themes of role of caste in politics. He studied caste from a historical perspective and later on from an integrative perspective. He even made comparisons of kinship in Indo-European cultures.

3. What are Ghurye's views on tribes? Elaborate.

Ans. Tribes are an integral part of Indian population. According to Ghurye separate identity of the tribals should be maintained and they should not be integrated with the mainstream of Indian society otherwise they would lose their own authentic identity.

He believed that the tribals were different from the non-tribals or Hindus. Also the tribals were the original inhabitants of India and unlike the Hindus they are the **animists.**

Ghurye advocated that the contact of tribals with non-tribals had been harmful for the culture and the economy of the tribals. In fact, some of the tribals lost their land and other resources to the greedy people. This was because some tribes have been integrated into the Indian society not knowing the real consequences.

4. Discuss the significance of religion according to Ghurye.

Ans. Ghurye made original contribution to the study of Indian religions, beliefs and practices. He wrote six books viz Gods and Men (1962), Indian Sadhus (1953), Religious Consciousness (1965), Indian Acculturation, Vedic India (1979), The Legacy of Ramayana (1979) to certify the role of religion in the society.

Ghurye has trace the outline of five foundations of culture that are

(i) religion

(ii consciousness

(iii) justice

(iv) free pursuit of knowledge

(v) toleration

Ghurye believed religious consciousness as a value that is manifested itself at the dawn of history.

5. Discuss about expanding horizons of Sociology.

Ans. Ghurye explored new domains of social and cultural life in India and the world. Out of which the important field was literature and the society. Ghurye became one of the first Indian sociologists to have utilised literature in sociological studies.

His vast knowledge of Sanskrit literature that was extensively quoted from the vedas, shastras, epics and the poetry of Kalidasa shed light on the social and cultural life of the Indians.

He made use of literature in vernacular like Marathi and cited modern writers from literature like Bankim Chandra Chatterjee. Scholars are of the view that Ghurye's knowledge was encyclopedic and his method was somewhat elective. The research and the writings opened up new avenues and dimensions in sociological inquiry of India.

6. Discuss the principle of purity and pollution control the caste system? Also discuss about the sharing of food among different caste members.

Ans. The concept of purity and pollution is the major aspect in understanding the hierarchy process of the caste system. Purity and pollution is also known as the basis of untouchability practice. In India, there were four varnas in which Brahmins hold the superior position and Shudras had the lowest position. There are elaborate rules based on the purity and pollution principle prescribing what kind of food may be shared among different cast members. The same principles applied to the institution of untouchability, social interaction, and even labour. Among the four dominant castes, the Brahmins are considered to be the purest.

In real practice, there is almost no objection to consumption of kuccha food or food cooked with water from a Brahmin. Higher caste can only take or consume pucca food or food cooked in butter from the lower caste. But nobody can take food or water from an untouchable whose touch is even considered to be polluting.

7. What does D.P. Mukerji mean by a 'living tradition'? Why did he insist that Indian sociologists be rooted in this tradition? **(NCERT)**

Ans. By 'living tradition', D.P. Mukerji means that the traditions were not only formed in the past but also kept on changing with the present and evolved over time. It manages to retain basic elements from the past.

He insisted that Indian sociologists be rooted in this tradition because an Indian sociologist should be an Indian first, which means that he/she should understand his/her social system first.

In Mukerji's words, "it is not enough for the Indian sociologist to be a sociologist. He must be an Indian first, that is, he is to share in the folk-ways, mores, customs and traditions, for the purpose of understanding his social system and what lies beneath it and beyond it."

In keeping with this view, he believed that sociologists should learn and be familiar with both 'high' and 'low' languages and cultures, not only Sanskrit, Persian or Arabic but also local dialects.

8. Discuss the restrictions on marriages under caste system.

Ans. In the caste system, there were many different restrictions on marriage . Firstly, there was prohibition of inter-caste marriage and people cannot marry outside their own caste and else they would practice endogamy. Ghurye mentioned the role of hypergamy (marrying a person of a superior caste or class) in promoting limited mobility within the caste system. In Gujarat and Rajasthan, there are instances where the kings have married tribal women.

Caste is also linked to kinship through caste endogamy and gotra endogamy. Gotra has been treated as a completely exogamous unit by the Brahmins and later by the non-Brahmins. The basic notion here is that all members of a gotra are related to one another through the lines of blood.

The fact that gotra survives even today with less exceptions shows that it can be tyrannical power of ideas and beliefs in human behaviour and social process.

9. What are the specificities of Indian culture and society and how do they affect the pattern of change?
(NCERT)

Ans. The Indian culture and society are not individualistic like the Western society. The behaviour of an Indian individual is fixed by his socio-cultural group. Hence, the Indian social system is oriented towards groups, unlike the Western societies where people are highly individualistic. The actions of individuals in Indian society are mostly involuntary. The traditions are strongly rooted in the past.

Thus, there are fewer changes in Indian societies, as the pattern of desires of an individual are mostly governed by the societal traditions and norms. Changes occur more in the adaptive form than any basic form. The role of economy as an internal source of change is diluted in the Indian society. Conflict due to caste system causes adaptive changes without overriding the institution of caste.

10. How a performance of a 'Welfare State' can be measured, according to A.R. Desai?

Ans. According to A.R. Desai, the test criteria against which the performance of the 'Welfare State' can be measured as follows

(i) Welfare state should ensure freedom from poverty, social discrimination and security for all its citizens.

(ii) Welfare state should remove inequalities of income through measures to redistribute income from the rich to the poor, and by preventing the concentration of wealth.

(iii) Welfare state should transform the economy in such a way that the capitalist profit motive is made **subservient** to the real needs of the community.

(iv) Welfare state should ensure stable development free from the cycle of economic booms and depressions.

(v) Welfare state should provide employment for all.

11. What is the significance of village studies in the history of Indian Sociology? What role did M.N. Srinivas play in promoting village studies?
(NCERT)

Ans. **Significance of Village Studies in Indian Sociology**

The study of Indian villages has always been important in the history of Indian Sociology because of the following reasons

(i) It provided with an opportunity to emphasis the importance of ethnographic research methods.

(ii) It provided examples of rapid social change that took place in the country after independence and implementation of planned development.

(*iii*) It enabled urban Indians and policy makers to form their opinions about developments in the villages of India.

Role of Srinivas in Promoting Village Studies

- MN Srinivas played a very important role in promoting village studies by concentrating his research on village areas.
- He conducted field work in villages and coordinated efforts at producing detailed ethnographic accounts of villages.
- His writings featured ethnographic accounts and historical and conceptual discussions about villages. He was critical of the arguments presented by the British anthropologists.
- He also presented the links of the village community to the economy of the outside world.

• Long Answer (LA) Type Questions

1. How did Ananthakrishna Iyer and Sarat Chandra Roy come to practice social anthropology?   **(NCERT)**

Ans. **Practice of Social Anthropology by Ananthakrishna Iyer** He came to practice social anthropology voluntarily by helping the British administrators in ethnographic surveys of India. He was initially a clerk and then became a college teacher at Ernakulum. In 1902, he was asked by the Dewan of Cochin to assist with an ethnographic survey of the state. Later, he worked for British government as unpaid Superintendent of Ethnography. His work received appreciation from British anthropologists and administrators.

Iyer became a reader at the University of Madras and set up the post-graduate department of anthropology at the University of Calcutta. Thus, he became the first self-taught anthropologist.

Practice of Social Anthropology by Sarat Chandra Roy He was educated in law and English. He gave up his law practice and became a school teacher in Ranchi. He was appointed as the official interpreter in the court after he resumed his law practice.

Gradually, he became interested in the tribal society, as he had to interpret the tribal customs in the court. He gained considerable knowledge on the culture and society of the tribal people of Chhotanagpur. Roy produced valuable monographs and research articles on this subject. He travelled and did intensive fieldwork pertaining to the tribal community.

Thus, the experiences gained by Iyer and Roy in the course of their work led to their interest in social anthropology.

2. What were the main arguments on either side of the debate about how to relate to tribal communities?   **(NCERT)**

Ans. The main arguments, on either side of the debate about relating to tribal communities, were led by the British administrator-anthropologists and the nationalists.

According to British Thinkers

According to the British, the tribes of India were primitive people and had a different culture from the Hindus.

They believed that the simple tribal people would suffer exploitation and cultural degradation at the hands of Hindu people who wanted the assimilation of tribal people with them. Thus, they needed to be protected by the state in order to safeguard their interests.

According to Indian Thinkers

On the other hand, the nationalists, of whom G.S. Ghurye was the most famous exponent, argued that the tribes of India were not backward, but had been interacting with the rest of Hindu society over a long period. The process of assimilation had been experienced by all the communities in India and the tribes were only a step behind in this process.

According to nationalists, attempts to preserve tribal culture only contributed to their backwardness. They believed tribal society needed as much reform as Hindu society.

Thus, the main difference in both the viewpoints was the perception about the impact of mainstream culture on tribes.

3. Write Ghurye's views about rural and urban areas.

Ans. Govind Sadashiv Ghurye's views about rural and urban areas are as follows

(i) The function of the city is to perform a culturally integrative role, where it acts as a point of focus and the centre which shows major principles of different periods.

(ii) Not any city, but large city or metropolis having an organic link with the life of the people of its region can do this work well.

(iii) According to Ghurye, any urban planner must tackle the problems of

   (a) Lack of sufficient supply of drinking water
   (b) Human congestion
   (c) Traffic congestion,
   (d) Regulation of public vehicles
   (e) Insufficiency of railway transport in cities like Mumbai
   (f) Deforestation
   (g) Noise pollution
   (h) Growth of slums
   (i) Plight of the pedestrians.

(vi) G.S. Ghurye was a **staunch** advocate of urbanisation. He, however, remained preoccupied for life with the idea of urbanisation securing the advantages of urban life simultaneously with nature's greenery.

(v) Urbanisation in India was not a simple function of industrialisation. A large city of metropolis also functioned as the centre of culture of the territory encompassing it.

(vi) The organic link between the urban centres and the villages was ignored during the British rule. Towns and cities began functioning as centres for producing industrial goods and for marketing industrial products made in India or in the UK to the rural masses.

4. Discuss views of D.P. Mukerji about Tradition and Modernity.

Ans. D.P. Mukerji's views on Traditions

He argued that traditions also change with social change. The principles of change are recognised in Indian tradition are *Shruti*, *Smriti* and *Anubhava*. Among these, *Anubhava* is a revolutionary principle. Many upanishads are based on it. Traditions perform the act of preserving but they are not essentially conservative. Personal experience of the saints/founders of different sects or panths flourished into collective experience.

It produced change in the social order. The experience of love (prem) and spontaneity (sahaj) of these saints and followers can be seen in sufis among the Muslims. The power of the Indian tradition lies in crystalisation of values emerging from past events in the life-habits/emotions of men and women. According to Mukerji, our country has preserved many values. Due to this, many Indian traditions are utilising the foreign forces.

D.P. Mukerji's views on Modernity

For modernity, Mukerji argued that adjustment between traditional and modern values will certainly take place in the Indian society. Western culture has touched Indians. Our present modern culture has enough flexibility to assimilate tribal and foreign culture. So, living in adjustment is in the blood of Indians.

They have developed Hindu-Muslim cultures and blending modern Indian cultures. Mukerji does not worship tradition. His idea of 'full man' or 'well balanced personality' demands blend of moral and intellectual sense of history and rationality. He also argued that a dialectical process of conflict and synthesis must be promoted by class structure of modern Indian society.

5. Outline the positions of Herbert Risley and G.S. Ghurye on the relationship between race and caste in India.   **(NCERT)**

Ans. Position of Herbert Risley on the relationship between race and caste is as follows

- Herbert Risley believed that human beings could be divided into separate races on the basis of their physical characteristics.
- His main argument was that caste originated in race because the different castes belonged to different racial types.
- He believed that the higher castes originated from Indo-Aryans while the lower castes originated from non-Aryan race.
- Risley had the opinion that the conditions in India were suitable for studying racial evolution as inter-caste marriages was strictly prohibited in India.

Position of GS Ghurye on the relationship between race and caste is as follows

- Ghurye was of a different view. He believed that Risley's argument was partially correct and the argument of upper castes being Aryan and lower castes being non-Aryan was true only for North India.
- He further said that the prohibition of intermixing of different castes was only limited to the Northern India, and people in other areas had been mixing for a long time.

According to him, racial purity was preserved only in North India while other parts adopted the practice of endogamy only after variations had occurred in racial groups.

6. Discuss in detail the contribution and the role played by the new class i.e. middle class, in the context of Indian society according to the viewpoint or standpoint of D.P. Mukerji.

Ans. According to D.P. Mukerji, following are the roles of new middle class

(i) The urban industrial order was introduced by the British in India and it set aside the older institutional networks. It also led to the dissolution of several traditional caste and classes. It called for a new kind of social adaptation and adjustment.

(ii) In the new set-up, the educated middle class of the urban centres of India became the main focal point of the society.

(iii) The new middle class of India came to command the knowledge of the modern social forces which was in terms of science and technology, democracy and a new sense of historical development which was prevalent in the West.

(iv) The new society that emerged in India called for utilisation of impressive qualities and the useful service of the new middle class people.

(v) The new emerging middle class was full of Western ideas and lifestyles and they have remained more contended and blissful as significant parts of Indian culture and Indian reality.

(vi) India with the help of this newly emerged middle class moved on the road to modernisation and also established the link with the masses.

(vii) The people of the middle class brought many new associated values with them that helped Indian grow holistically. These middle class generally belonged to varied professions like doctors, engineers, etc.

(viii) Slowly, India got enriched by this new experience of the middle class that gave so much towards the building up of the nation as a one entity.

7. What is a welfare state? Why is A.R. Desai critical of the claims made on its behalf? **(NCERT)**

Ans. **Meaning of Welfare State** A.R. Desai explained welfare state among following three features

(i) A welfare state is a positive state that uses its power in order to implement social policies for the betterment of society. It is interventionist in nature.

(ii) Democracy and democratic institutions are considered the most important factors for the emergence of the welfare state.

(iii) A welfare state includes a mixed economy. It means the co-existence of both the private and state owned enterprises. The public sector concentrates on basic goods and social infrastructure, while the private industry produces consumer goods.

Critical Claims of A.R. Desai on Welfare State

- Desai is critical of welfare states like Britain, USA and countries in Europe.
- He argues that the claims of these states are not real.
- They are not even able to provide basic social and economic security to their citizens. They are unable to reduce economic inequality.
- The process of development in these states is not independent of market fluctuations.
- A high level of unemployment alongside excess economic capacity indicates the failure of welfare state.

Therefore, AR Desai is critical of the claims made on behalf of welfare state and concludes that its existence is a myth.

8. Read the following passage and answer the question that follow.

Ananthakrishna Iyer was probably the first self-taught anthropologist to receive national and international recognition as a scholar and an academician. He was invited to lecture at the University of Madras, and was appointed as a reader at the University of Calcutta, where he helped set up the first post-graduate anthropology department in India. He remained at the University of Calcutta from 1917 to 1932. Though he had no formal qualifications in anthropology, he was elected President of the Ethnology section of the Indian Science Congress. He was awarded an honorary doctorate by a German University during his lecture tour of European universities. He was also conferred the titles of Rai Bahadur and Dewan Bahadur by Cochin State.

Who was Ananthakrishna Iyer? What are the achievements of Ananthakrishna Iyer in the field of anthropology? How did the world recognise his talent and what could be learnt from his life?

Ans. Ananthakrishna Iyer was one of the self-taught anthropologists who gained national and international recognition as a scholar and academician. He is one of the pioneers of social anthropology in India. Iyer gained attention from the ethnographic studies which he conducted in India during British rule.

The achievements of Ananthakrishna Iyer in the field of anthropology are mentioned below

- He was appointed as a reader at the University of Calcutta, where he helped to set up the first post-graduate anthropology department in India.
- He was elected as the President of the Ethnology section of the Indian Science Congress.
- He was also awarded the honorary doctorate by a German University during his lecture tour of European Universities.

The world learned to recognised the talent of Ananthakrishna Iyer through the contributions he made in the field of social anthropology without any formal training at that. The ethnographies he conducted in India contributed to this recognition. He was awarded an honorary doctorate as he was recognised as an international scholar. His great interest in anthropology paved the way to the establishment of the same as a formal discipline when such a discipline was non-existent in India.

9. Read the following passage and answer the question that follow.

Conflict and rebellion in the Indian context have tended to work through collective experiences. But the resilience of tradition ensures that the pressure of conflict produces change in the tradition without breaking it. So, we have repeated cycles of dominant orthodoxy being challenged by popular revolts which succeed in transforming orthodoxy, but are eventually reabsorbed into this transformed tradition. This process of change of rebellion contained within the limits of an overarching tradition is typical of a caste society, where the formation of classes and class consciousness has been inhibited. D.P.'s views on tradition and change led him to criticise all instances of unthinking borrowing from Western intellectual traditions, including in such contexts as development planning. Tradition was neither to be worshipped nor ignored, just as modernity was needed but not to be blindly adopted. DP was simultaneously a proud but critical inheritor of tradition, as well as an admiring critic of the modernity that he acknowledged as having shaped his own intellectual perspective.

What do you understand by conflict and rebellion in Indian context? What is tradition according to the passage? Why does a society challenge dominant orthodoxy?

Ans. Conflict and rebellion tend to work together, but it ensures that the changes produce as the result of conflict generates changes in the tradition without breaking it. Many orthodox ideas have been challenged by revolutionary conflicts, transforming the orthodox ideas in the process.

Tradition refers to the process of the transfer of beliefs and customs from one generation to another. Tradition helps to shape the social behaviour of individuals and some traditions are passed from one generation to another through the word of mouth. D.P. Mukerji's views on tradition and change led him to criticise all instances of blind borrowings of intellectual traditions from Western society.

Society challenges the dominant orthodoxy as there is inacceptance of orthodoxy ideas in the society. Hence, through rebellion and conflict, these ideas are challenged and orthodoxy is transformed.

• Case Based Questions

1. Read the following passage and answer the questions.

Conflict and rebellion in the Indian context have tended to work through collective experiences. But the resilience of tradition ensures that the pressure of conflict produces a change in the tradition without breaking it. So, we have repeated cycles of dominant orthodoxy being challenged by popular revolts which succeed in transforming orthodoxy but are eventually reabsorbed into this transformed tradition. This process of change — of rebellion contained within the limits of an overarching tradition — is typical of a caste society, where the formation of classes and class consciousness has been inhibited. D.P.'s views on tradition and change led him to criticise all instances

of unthinking borrowing from Western intellectual traditions, including in such contexts as development planning. Tradition was neither to be worshipped nor ignored, just as modernity was needed but not to be blindly adopted.

(i) What makes the change produced due to conflict in a cast society unique?

Ans. The process of change is unique in caste society because the conflict causes change or rebellion contained within the bounds of tradition without breaking it.

(ii) Is it valid to say, the presence resilience of tradition to the changes caused by conflict prevents the tradition from being broken? If so, why?

Ans. Yes, it's valid to say the presence resilience of tradition to the changes caused by conflict prevents the same from being broken. Because the change transforms the tradition and gets absorbed in the same.

(iii) As a Marxist, did D.P. Mukerji believed that class conflict and class consciousness could be formed in Indian society? If so/not so, why?

Ans. D.P. Mukerji believed that class conflict and class consciousness could not be formed in the Indian caste society, because of the empowering role traditions or caste traditions.

2. Read the following passage carefully and answer questions.

He examines the performance of those states that are most often described as welfare states, such as Britain, the USA, and much of Europe, and finds their claims to be greatly exaggerated. Thus, most modern capitalist states, even in the most developed countries, fail to provide minimum levels of economic and social security to all their citizens. They are unable to reduce economic inequality and often seem to encourage it. The so-called welfare states have also been unsuccessful at enabling stable development free from market fluctuations. The presence of excess economic capacity and high levels of unemployment is yet another failure.

(i) Whom does 'he' in the above passage imply to? Which perspective was used by this person to analyse the concept of state?

Ans. 'He in' the above passage implies to A.R. Desai. He was highly influenced by the Marxist perspective and used the same to analyse the concept of state.

(ii) Why, as per Desai, the well-known welfare states are not eligible for that title?

Ans. According to Desai most of the well-known welfare states fail to provide minimum levels of economic, social security and reduce economic inequality among the citizens. Thus, they are not eligible for the title of the welfare state.

(iii) List the three core features of a welfare state Desai highlighted through his contribution to Indian Sociology?

Ans. Desai provided the following three features of a welfare state. These are as follows
A welfare state is positive and interventionist.
A welfare state is a democratic state.
A welfare state has a mixed economy.

3. Read the following passage carefully and answer the questions.

He was invited to lecture at the University of Madras, and was appointed as a reader at the University of Calcutta, where he helped set up the first post-graduate anthropology department in India. He remained at the University of Calcutta from 1917 to 1932. Though, he had no formal qualifications in anthropology, he was elected President of the Ethnology section of the Indian Science Congress. He was awarded an honorary doctorate by a German University during his lecture tour of European universities. He was also conferred the titles of Rao Bahadur and Dewan Bahadur by Cochin State.

(i) Who is "he" in the above-mentioned passage? What is the common term associating "he" and Sarat Chandra Roy?

Ans. He in the above-mentioned passage is L.K. Ananthakrishna Iyer. The common term associating him with Sarat Chandra Roy is an accidental anthropologist.

(ii) Ananthakrishna Iyer was a self-taught anthropologist. Is this statement valid and why?

Ans. Yes, this statement is valid because Iyer had no formal education in anthropology yet he was probably the first self-taught anthropologist to receive national and international recognition as a scholar and an academician.

(iii) Is it valid to say, Ananthakrishan Iyer, like M.N. Srinivas, lived and practiced social anthropology in British-ruled India? Why?

Ans. No, it's not valid to say that Iyer, like Srinivas, lived and practiced social anthropology in British ruled India because, unlike Iyer, Srinivas practiced Sociology in independent India.

Chapter Test

Multiple Choice Questions

1. Which of the following is not the feature of caste defined by Ghurye?
   (a) Segmental division
   (b) Equal opportunity
   (c) Restrictions on marriage
   (d) Hierarchical division

2. Who believed that there were three principles of change recognised in Indian tradition namely Shruti, Smriti and Anubhava.
   (a) D.P. Mukerji
   (b) Sarat Chandra Roy
   (c) A.R. Desai
   (d) Ghurye

3. In 1920, two other universities i.e., Calcutta and ____ began programmes of teaching and research in sociology and ____ .
   (a) Lucknow, anthropology
   (b) Bombay, anthropology
   (c) Madras, anthropology
   (d) Delhi, anthropology

4. ____ was given the titles of Rao Bahadur and Dewan Bahadur by the ____ state.
   (a) G.S. Ghurye, Bombay
   (b) S.C. Dube, Calcutta·
   (c) Sarat Chandra Roy, Madras
   (d) Anathakrishna Iyer, Cochin

5. ____ journal was founded by Sarat Chandra Roy in ____ .
   (a) Man in Society, 1921
   (b) Man in India, 1922
   (c) Man in Indian Society, 1922
   (d) Man in Wild, 1921

Short Answer Type Questions

6. Discuss A.R. Desai's view about the state.

7. Discuss the changes that M.N. Srinivas observed in the Indian villages?

8. Discuss the ways of classification of the writings of Srinivas.

9. What do you understand by endogamy and exogamy?

10. Summarise the social anthropological definition of caste.

Long Answer Type Questions

11. What are the specificities of Indian culture and society and how do they affect the pattern of change?

12. What arguments were given for and against the village as a subject of sociological research by M.N. Srinivas and Louis Dumont?

13. What are the structural features of caste as given by Ghurye?

Answers

1. (b)   *2.* (a)   *3.* (a)   *4.* (d)   *5.* (b)

Practice Papers
1-3

Practice Paper 1[*]
(Solved)

General Instructions

- Time : **2 Hours**
- Max. Marks : **40**

1. There are 10 questions in the question paper. All questions are compulsory.
2. Question no. 1 is a Case Based Question, which has five MCQs. Each question carries one mark.
3. Question no. 2-6 are Short Answer Type Questions. Each question carries 3 marks.
4. Question no. 7-10 are Long Answer Type Questions. Each question carries 5 marks.
5. There is no overall choice. However, internal choice have been provided in some questions.
   Students have to attempt only one of the alternatives in such questions.

** As exact Blue-print and Pattern for CBSE Term II exams is not released yet. So the pattern of this paper is designed by the author on the basis of trend of past CBSE Papers. Students are advised not to consider the pattern of this paper as official. It is just for practice purpose.*

Case Based Questions

1. Read the following passage and answer the five questions accordingly:

Sometimes changes in the economic organisation that are not directly technological can also change society. In a well-known historical example, plantation agriculture, it created a heavy demand for labour. This demand helped to establish the institution of slavery and the slave trade between Africa, Europe and the America between the 17th and 19th centuries. In India, too, the tea plantations of Assam involved the forced migration of labour from Eastern India (specially the Adivasi areas of Jharkhand and Chhattisgarh). Today, in many parts of the world, changes in customs duties or tariffs brought about by international agreements and institutions like the World Trade Organisation, can lead to entire industries and occupations being wiped out or (less often) sudden booms or periods of prosperity for other industries or occupations. $(1 \times 5 = 5)$

(i) Plantation agriculture is closely associated with which kind of crops?

   (a) Cash Crops   (b) Mono Crops   (c) Rabi   (d) Kharif

(ii) This passage is inferring to which kind of social change?

   (a) Technological change   (b) Economic change

   (c) Political change   (d) Both (a) and (b)

(iii) As per the given passage, slavery was based on ______ because it created a heavy demand for_______.

   (a) Agriculture, crops   (b) Plantation agriculture, crops

   (c) Agriculture, labour   (d) Plantation agriculture, labour

(iv) In India, the tea plantation of Assam led to which of the following?

   (a) Migration of people   (b) Migration of people from Eastern India

   (c) Migration of labour from Eastern India   (d) Migration of labour

(v) The institution of slavery led to the slave trade between which three nations?
    (a) Africa, Europe, United Kingdom   (b) Africa, Europe, United States of America
    (c) Africa, U.K., America   (d) U.K., America, Europe

Short Answer Type Questions
(5 × 3 = 15)

2. When was the Journal 'Man in India' founded, and by whom? Why is the founder of this journal important? (3)

Or Which debate popularized Ghurye outside the academic world? What was his position in this debate?

3. Who were considered as not fully evolved human beings during the age of reason? (3)

4. How did the historical circumstances of the Second World War help women with their struggle for equality? (3)

5. Why did D.P. Mukerji call collective anubhava the driving force of change in Indian society? (3)

Or Which class conflict prevalent in Indian society as per D.P. Mukerji? Give reason for your answer.

6. A separation was built between the public and private spheres. Justify this statement with reference to the French Revolution. (3)

Or Why did Marx believe that capitalism was a necessary stage even with its drawbacks?

Long Answer Type Questions
(4 × 5 = 20)

7. Which classical Indian sociologist provided a comprehensive view on caste? Illuminate the features of caste put forward by this sociologist. (5)

Or What is a welfare state? How did A.R. Desai break the myth of the welfare states?

8. Explain in detail how Marx believed socialism would be obtained? And why was capitalism necessary for this future he saw? (5)

9. How did Max Weber define authority? With the aid of examples, differentiate between the kinds of authority? (5)

Or How is social order maintained in rural and urban settings? What is the scope of social change in these settings?

10. Differentiate between primitive and modern society from the perspective of Emile Durkheim. (5)

Or In detail, explain how social facts and social actions are different from one another? Mention five points that are causing them to differ.

Answers

1. (i) (a) The plantation agriculture is closely associated with cash crops like sugarcane, tea, and cotton. Plantation agriculture involved the plantation of single cash crops in enhancing their production.

  (ii) (b) This passage infers to the economic change that was brought on by plantation agriculture.

  (iii) (d) As per the given passage, slavery was based on plantation agriculture because it created a heavy demand for labour.

  (iv) (c) In India, the tea plantation of Assam led to the migration of labour from Eastern India to meet the demand for cultivation and plantation demand.

  (v) (b) The institution of slavery led to the slave trade between Africa, Europe, and America between the 17th and 19th centuries.

2. The Journal Man in India was founded by Sarat Chandra Roy in 1922. The founder of this journal, i.e., Sarat Chandra Roy, is a very significant figure in Indian sociology for the following reasons

- He is considered one of the pioneers who paved the way for the establishment of Indian sociology. He practised social anthropology who fits the label of an accidental anthropologist.

- He conducted monographs on tribes of India before anthropology was established as a formal discipline in India. Man in India is the first journal of its kind which is still printed.

- He wrote over 100 articles in leading Indian and British journals.

Or

The debate with Verrier Elwin made Ghurye famous outside the academic world. This debate was based on how the State should respond to the position of tribals in Indian society. Elwin was the proponent of the dominant position or protectionist view who believed the State should try to protect the tribes and their distinct culture, which was facing pressure to assimilate into mainstream culture. Ghurye opposed this view and adopted a nationalist position. He claimed that tribes and their cultures should assimilate into the mainstream culture because preventing this assimilation would further enhance their backwardness. He called them backward Hindus and claimed most of them have already interacted and been exposed to mainstream culture.

3. During the age of reason or enlightenment period, those individuals who could'nt reason or think were considered not evolved. Enlightenment or the age of reason placed rationality or the ability to reason at the centre. Humans ability to think or reason made them the producers as well as the consumers of the knowledge. Society, being the handiwork of humans, could be comprehended, understood, and analysed by humans through rational and critical thinking. Therefore, those who could'nt reason or think were considered unevolved, like in the case of primitive savages.

   Enlightenment had a huge role to play in establishing sociology as a discipline. The French Revolution and the Industrial Revolution that followed were marked by the age of reason. Rational thinking replaced the traditional ways of thinking where people understood society through the perspective of religion.

4. The historical circumstances of the Second World War helped women with their struggle for equality in the following ways.

   - As a result of the Second World War, women in the western countries started working in factories and carrying out the tasks and duties performed by only men.
   - During this time, women started building ships, operating heavy machinery, manufacturing armaments, and so on.
   - As a result of the Second World War, women were treated equally when they carried the work only done by men before. This helped them in their struggle for equality.
   - Before World War II, women were mostly stuck at home taking care of household needs. During the II World War, when men went to war, women entered the workforce and contributed to the economy, and led a civilian life.

5. D.P. Mukerji called collective or generalised anubhava the driving force of change in Indian society because of the following reasons

   - D.P. Mukerji argued that Indian society's most distinctive feature was its social system. The tradition was a huge part of Indian culture. Due to the emphasis he placed on tradition and culture, D.P. argued that there is three driving force of change in Indian society, namely, shruti, smriti, and anubhava. Anubhava or personal experience is the most important among them.
   - The Indian culture and tradition, unlike the Western society, gave importance to the collective instead of the individual. Indian culture, which was deep-rooted in traditions, was based on macro-level institutions like caste or religion. This inclination prioritised collective anubhava over personal anubhava as the generalized anubhava dominated the Indian society.

Or

The class conflict was not prevalent in Indian society as per D.P. Mukerji.

   - D.P. Mukerji believed that the caste traditions in India covered the class conflict in Indian society.
   - The emergence of new class and class relations was prevented due to the overarching impact of caste traditions in Indian society.
   - Being a Marxist, he claimed that, unlike in the case of western society, the economic causes should not be stressed as a factor of internal change in India because the non-economic factors such as caste or tradition were more important factors of change in the context of Indian society.

6. A separation was built between the public, and private realm is justifiable from the background of the French Revolution. This statement could be justified on the following grounds

   - The French Revolution introduced the idea of political sovereignty and nation-state for the first time. When the peasants rose against the elites and broke free from their exploitative feudal lords stressed the idea of freedom or free citizens.
   - The French Revolution emphasised people as free citizens of the republic and sovereign individuals who had their own rights and were equal before the law and other institutions of the state.
   - This notion established a separation between the private realm of the household and the public realm of the state.

Or

Karl Marx believed that capitalism was a necessary stage even with its drawbacks due to the following reasons

   - Capitalism was needed, according to Marx, to lead the way for a socialist society. The exploitation and alienation resulting from capitalism was the driving force for the class to emerge.

- Marx believed the class consciousness was not possible without capitalism. The working class will not rise and identify their collective struggle and cause for the class consciousness to be developed.
- Ultimately the class consciousness would lead to class struggle paving the way for revolution resulting in a socialist society, as per Marx.

7. G.S. Ghurye, one of the classical Indian sociologists, provided a comprehensive view on caste. He worked on various themes, but his detailed definition of caste is considered important in Indian sociology. Ghurye pointed out six features of caste in an attempt to explain it. These six features are as follows

- Caste is an institution based on segmental division. This means that caste is divided into a number of closed, mutually exclusive segments or compartments. Each caste is one such compartment. It is closed because caste is decided by birth at birth, it can neither be avoided nor changed.
- Caste is based on hierarchical division. Each caste is strictly unequal to every other caste, i.e., every caste is either higher or lower than every other one.
- The institution of caste necessarily involves restrictions on social interaction, especially the sharing of food. These rules are governed by ideas of purity and pollution.
- Caste also involves differential rights and duties for different castes. These rights and duties pertain not only to religious practices but extend to the secular world.
- Caste restricts the choice of occupation. It involves a rigid form of the division of labour with specific occupations allocated based on specific castes.
- Caste involves strict restrictions on marriage. Caste 'endogamy', or marriage only within the caste, is often accompanied by rules about 'exogamy' or whom one may not marry.

Or

A welfare state is defined by A.R. Desai based on certain features it should possess. These are as follows:

- A welfare state is a positive state, where the state does not only do the bare minimum to maintain law and order. Instead, a welfare state is an interventionist State enforcing laws and social policy for the betterment of society.
- A welfare state is a democratic state. Democracy is essential for a welfare state to function. And it's a democracy involving multi-party elections, unlike the socialist or communist states.

- A welfare state has a mixed economy. It means the economy where both private capitalist enterprises and State or publicly owned enterprises co-exist. A welfare state does not seek to eliminate the capitalist market, nor does it prevent public investment in industry and other fields.

A.R. Desai broke the myth of the welfare state and argued that most nations claiming to be welfare states fail to meet the criteria for the same. Based on the following parameters, they broke the myth of the welfare state

- He checked if a welfare state ensures freedom from poverty, social discrimination, and security for its citizens. Does it promote equal income by distributing the wealth equally among different sections of society?
- Does the State ensure equal employment to all accompanied by stable development 'free from economic boom and depression? Also, he checked if the State puts the capitalist profit is made subservient to the real needs of the community.

8. Karl Marx believed that socialism would be obtained in the following manner

- He argued that the accentuating alienation and exploitation witnessed in a capitalist society would pave the way for socialism.
- The mode of production and the relations of production in capitalist society create two distinct classes, i.e., bourgeoisie and proletariat. The working class would realise their collective class situation, and exploitation faced under capitalism would create class consciousness.
- Class consciousness of the working class would ultimately lead to class struggle resulting in revolution and overthrowing capitalism paving the way for socialism.

Karl Marx believed capitalism was necessary for the socialist society he saw as the future because of the following

- Without capitalism, there would be no class emergence and class formation. The alienation and exploitation faced under the capitalist regime resulted in the formation of a class-based economy.
- Capitalism is also necessary for the class consciousness to develop so that the working class identifies their collective and similar class condition leading to class struggle.
- The revolution will not take place without the presence of capitalism. Therefore, its deemed necessary for socialism to arise.

9. Max Weber defines authority as a kind of power that is legitimate, just or proper, justified or proper. For instance, a police officer, a judge, or a school teacher all exercise different kinds of authority as part of their jobs. This authority is explicitly provided to them by their official job description, there are written documents specifying their authority and what they may and may not do. Authority automatically invites obedience. The authority wielded by a judge makes everyone obey him/her in the courtroom.

Authority can take two different manifestations, these are as follows

Formal or Formalised Authority	Non-formalised Authority
A formalised authority has officially stated rules and laws associated with it.	A non-formalsied authority does not have any official rules or laws associated with it.
Formalised authority is transparent when it comes to rules and regulations defining the same.	Non-formal authority may have invisible or implicit rules or laws defining the same.
Formalised authority controls the action of individuals. People abide by the formalised authority.	Non-formalised authority also controls the actions of people through the power exerted by individual or person.
Law and order is an example of formalised authority. For example, the authority wielded by a judge is defined by transparent laws and rules attached to the job description of the judge. Law controls the actions of people.	The authority wielded by a leader of a sect could be an example of non-formalised authority. A sect leader can control the activities of the individual. There are no written rules or laws dictating his authority. Like law, the authority of a sect leader is not codified.

Or

Social order is maintained in rural and urban setting in the following manner

Rural Setting or Village

- The power structure and the social structure of rural setting plays a vital role in maintaining the social order. The traditional power structure based institutions like caste, religion and other forms of customary or traditional social practice are stronger here.
- This leads to the domination of the upper or dominant caste over others reaffirming the social order already in place.
- The relative power of the dominant sections is much more as they control most avenues of employment and most resources. So the poor have to depend on the dominant sections since there are no alternative sources of employment or support. Given the small population,

it is also very difficult to gather large numbers, particularly since efforts towards this cannot be hidden from the powerful and are very quickly suppressed.

Urban Setting or City

- Unlike rural regions, urban areas or cities are the domain of modernity. Here modern ways of thinking dominate the social fabric of society.
- A city is also a domain of mass politics packed with a large and dense population. This composition established the notion of anonymity in the city. City, unlike the village, nurtures individuals.
- Social order is a result of constraints faced by individuals through their group identities. The economic and social constraints imposed by membership in group identities — based on factors like race, religion, ethnicity, caste, region, and of course, the class proved vital in establishing social order.

The scope of change is more prevalent in an urban setting than in a rural setting. Changes occur at a slower pace in villages compared to the cities, and this creates a cultural lag.

10. The differences between the modern and primitive society from the viewpoint of Emile Durkheim are as follows

Primitive or Traditional Society	Modern Society
In primitive society, there is strong mechanical solidarity among its members. This solidarity is based on the homogenous nature of society and its members.	In modern society, organic solidarity is prevalent among the members of society. This solidarity is based on differences and the heterogenous nature of society and its members.
The community feeling is strong in primitive society, and people are well integrated into the society.	The community feeling is not as strong as the primitive society here. Individuals take precedence over the collective here.
The nature of law in this society is repressive. This implies that any violation of societal norms is met with harsh punishments.	The nature of law is restitutive. Instead of harsh punishments, modern society tends to correct the fault or mistakes of its member through the law.
The size of the population is relatively small and homogenous compared to modern society.	The size of the population is large and heterogeneous compared to the primitive society.
In primitive societies, social relationships are personal and close. The individual identifies with the collective society.	In this society, social relationships are impersonal and need-based. The individuals have a group identity.

Or

The difference between social facts and social actions are as follows

Social Facts	Social Action
Emile Durheim developed the concept of social facts.	Max Weber developed the concept of social action.
Social facts are things that are external to individuals exerting force over them.	Social actions, on the other hand, refer to the action of individuals with a meaning attached to this action.
Social facts represent the large-scale external realities like caste, religion, or culture controlling the action of individuals.	In comparison, social action micro-level reality of an individual.
Social facts passively overlook individuals as their significance.	Social action emphasises the role of individuals and gives them significance, unlike social fact.
Social facts could be utilised to study and analyse abstract social realities indirectly.	Social actions are utilised to understand the meaning attached to the action of individuals. It could be used to analyse individualistic actions.

Durkheim wanted to establish sociology as a formal empirical discipline. Through social facts, he wanted to prove that sociology could be a science used to analyse and study social problems and social realities. On the other hand, Max Weber wanted to bring a human touch to the discipline. He established interpretive sociology based on empathetic understanding. Social actions, as per him, should form the subject matter of sociology, along with focusing on the large-scale external social realities. The perspective of Durkheim and Weber was different, and this gave birth to their respective concepts of social facts and social action.

Practice Paper 2[*]

(Unsolved)

General Instructions

■ Time : **2 Hours**
■ Max. Marks : **40**

1. There are 10 questions in the question paper. All questions are compulsory.
2. Question no. 1 is a Case Based Question, which has five MCQs. Each question carries one mark.
3. Question no. 2-6 are Short Answer Type Questions. Each question carries 3 marks.
4. Question no. 7-10 are Long Answer Type Questions. Each question carries 5 marks.
5. There is no overall choice. However, internal choice have been provided in some questions. Students have to attempt only one of the alternatives in such questions.

** As exact Blue-print and Pattern for CBSE Term II exams is not released yet, so the pattern of this paper is designed by the author on the basis of trend of past CBSE Papers. Students are advised not to consider the pattern of this paper as official. It is just for practice purpose.*

Case Based Questions

1. Read the following passage and answer the five questions accordingly.

The moral codes were the key characteristics of a society that determined the behaviour patterns of individuals. Coming from a religious family, Durkheim cherished the idea of developing a secular understanding of religion. It was in his last book, The Elementary Forms of Religious Life that he was finally able to fulfil this wish. Society was for Durkheim a social fact which existed as a moral community over and above the individual. The ties that bound people in groups were crucial to the existence of society. These ties or social solidarities exerted pressure on individuals to conform to the norms and expectations of the group. This constrained the individual's behaviour pattern, limiting variation within a small range. Constriction of choice in social action meant that behaviour could now be predicted as it followed a pattern. So by observing behaviour patterns it was possible to identify the norms, codes and social solidarities which governed them. Thus, the existence of otherwise 'invisible' things like ideas, norms, values and so on could be empirically verified by studying the patterns of social behaviour of people as they related to each other in a society. $(1 \times 5 = 5)$

(i) Which sociologist considered that religion has a functional role in society?
  (a) Durkheim (b) Marx (c) Weber (d) Gramsci

(ii) Durkheim argued that the task of sociology should be the study of __________.
  (a) Social progress (b) Social facts (c) Anomie (d) Consciousness

(iii) Which of the following best describes anomie, as described by Durkheim?
  (a) A model that sociologists use to evaluate real-world
  (b) A society's loss of direction when social control of individual behaviour is ineffective
  (c) A research classification system
  (d) A mental disorder

(iv) According to Durkheim, the collective ways of thinking, feeling and acting is known as
    (a) Social integration   (b) Social solidarity
    (c) Social norms   (d) Social facts

(v) The term used by Durkheim to indicate the communal beliefs, morals and attitudes of a society is
_______________.
    (a) Collective morals   (b) Collective consciousness
    (c) Collective behaviour   (d) Collective conscience

Short Answer Type Questions

$(5 \times 3 = 15)$

2. How would you define the social anthropological definition of caste?   (3)

3. State a few causes of crime in the society.   (3)

Or "Society is not a static phenomenon, instead it is subject to constant change." Discuss.

4. What does Ghurye think about rural community and urban community?   (3)

Or What are the specificities of Indian culture and society according to DP Mukherjee?

5. Why is the Enlightenment period considered important for the development of Sociology?   (3)

Or What are the different stages of human society according to Marx?

6. Discuss Ghurye's views on tribes.   (3)

Long Answer Type Questions

$(4 \times 5 = 20)$

7. Explain in detail Karl Marx's theory of class struggle.   (5)

Or How did Durkheim explain "suicide"? Elaborate on the different types of suicides seen in society.

8. What arguments were given for and against the village as a subject of sociological research by M. N. Srinivas and Louis Dumont?   (5)

Or What does D.P. Mukherji mean by 'living tradition'? Why did he insist that Indian sociologists be rooted in this tradition?

9. Write a short note on the contribution of Max Weber to sociology.   (5)

10. Mention some features of the changes brought about by technology and the economy?   (5)

Or What is domination and how is it related to law and authority?

Answers

1.	(i) (a)	(ii) (b)	(iii) (b)	(iv) (d)	(v) (d)

Practice Paper 3[*]

(Unsolved)

<table>
<tr><td>

General Instructions

1. There are 10 questions in the question paper. All questions are compulsory.
2. Question no. 1 is a Case Based Question, which has five MCQs. Each question carries one mark.
3. Question no. 2-6 are Short Answer Type Questions. Each question carries 3 marks.
4. Question no. 7-10 are Long Answer Type Questions. Each question carries 5 marks.
5. There is no overall choice. However, internal choice have been provided in some questions. Students have to attempt only one of the alternatives in such questions.

</td><td>

■ Time : **2 Hours**
■ Max. Marks : **40**

</td></tr>
</table>

** As exact Blue-print and Pattern for CBSE Term II exams is not released yet, so the pattern of this paper is designed by the author on the basis of trend of past CBSE Papers. Students are advised not to consider the pattern of this paper as official. It is just for practice purpose.*

Case Based Questions

1. Read the following passage and answer the five questions accordingly

This term was made famous by the natural scientist Charles Darwin, who proposed a theory of how living organisms evolve – or change slowly over several centuries or even millenia, by adapting themselves to natural circumstances. Darwin's theory emphasised the idea of 'the survival of the fittest' – only those life forms manage to survive who are best adapted to their environment; those that are unable to adapt or are too slow to do so die out in the long run. Darwin suggested that human beings evolved from sea-borne life forms (or varieties of fish) to land-based mammals, passing through various stages the highest of which were the various varieties of monkeys and chimpanzees until finally the homo sapiens or human form was evolved. Although Darwin's theory referred to natural processes, it was soon adapted to the social world and was termed 'Social Darwinism', a theory that emphasised the importance of adaptive change. In contrast to evolutionary change, change that occurs comparatively quickly, even suddenly, is sometimes called 'revolutionary change'. It is used mainly in the political context, when the power structure of society changes very rapidly through the overthrow of a former ruling class or group by its challengers. Examples include the French revolution (1789-93) and the Soviet or Russian revolution of 1917. $(5 \times 1 = 5)$

(i) Which thinker proposed a theory where living organisms evolve-or change slowly over several centuries or even millennia, by adapting themselves to natural circumstances.

   (a) Spencer   (b) Darwin   (c) Einstein   (d) Comte

(ii) Youth rebellion is an example of ______ culture.

   (a) adaptive   (b) societal

   (c) counter   (d) revolutionary

(iii) Which term refers to an explicitly codified norm or rule?

   (a) Tariffs   (b) Law   (c) Authority   (d) Evolution

(iv) The French revolution(1789-93) and the Soviet or Russian revolution of 1917 are examples of ________ .
    (a) Evolution
    (b) Political evolution
    (c) Social evolution
    (d) Revolution

(v) Social Darwinism, is a theory that emphasised the importance of ______ change.
    (a) revolutionary
    (b) adaptive
    (c) evolutionary
    (d) societal

Short Answer Type Questions

$(5 \times 3 = 15)$

2. Mention Ghurye's contribution to sociology. (3)

Or What was D.P. Mukherji's view about traditions and modernity?

3. Briefly explain social facts as interpreted by Durkheim. (3)

Or List the suitable grounds on which Marxian theory of class struggle has been criticised.

4. How does the environment affect social change? Discuss. (3)

Or What are the ways to achieve social order?

5. Differentiate between rural and urban communities. (3)

6. Discuss main contributions of Max Weber. (3)

Or Differentiate between the sacred and the profane. Who gave these terms?

Long Answer Type Questions

$(5 \times 4 = 20)$

7. Discuss the factors that brought about social changes in society. (5)

Or Outline the positions of Herbert Risley and G.S. Ghurye on the relationship between race and caste in India.

8. Explain "theory of suicide" as stated by Emile Durkheim. (5)

Or Highlight the basic characteristics of religion.

9. How do demographic factors, education and social legislation cause social change? (5)

Or What is meant by social order? Is it maintained in urban areas? Discuss.

10. How did Max Weber explain "social action"? Elaborate on the types of social action seen in society. (5)

Answers

1.	*(i)* *(b)*	*(ii)* *(c)*	*(iii)* *(b)*	*(iv)* *(d)*	*(v)* *(b)*

Printed by Libri Plureos GmbH in Hamburg,
Germany